RICHMOND VIRGINIA AND THE TITANIC

WALTER S. GRIGGS JR.

THE History PRESS

Published by The History Press
Charleston, SC 29403
www.historypress.net

Front cover, top: Courtesy of Wikimedia Commons.

First published 2015

Manufactured in the United States

ISBN 978.1.62619.890.6

Library of Congress Control Number: 2014957210

Dedicated to my wife, Frances Pitchford Griggs,
and to my daughter, Cara Frances Griggs

Contents

Acknowledgements

This book would not have been written but for the fact that my brother Bob gave me a reproduction *Titanic* compass for Christmas. When I looked at it, I remembered how much I enjoyed studying the *Titanic* and decided to write a book explaining how Richmonders learned about and responded to the disaster.

In doing the research for the book, I relied heavily on the expertise of the archive staff at the Library of Virginia. I especially want to thank Minor Weisiger for directing me to some little-known sources.

I also want to thank the United States Coast Guard for providing me with pictures and manuscripts and the Wesleyan Class at Reveille United Methodist Church for giving me a book on the *Titanic* and a coffee cup. Both of these gifts proved to be extremely useful.

Since I have never learned how to use a digital camera with any degree of expertise, I want to thank my daughter, Cara, for helping me with every aspect of photography. Without her help, this book would have no pictures.

My wife, Frances Pitchford Griggs, proofread this book numerous times. Without her help and expertise, the entire book idea would have sunk like the *Titanic*. My advice to any writer is to marry an English major who enjoys grammar and listen to what they tell you.

Writing can sometimes be lonely and discouraging. I want to thank the following people for their moral support: Bob and Sue Griggs, Jill Kramer, Linda Pontius, Marianne Miller, Mike Tharp, Jason Chan, Elliott "Chip" Minor, Glenn Gilbreath, Jerry Becker, Susan Robbins, Bob Wood, Pat and Dick Harwood, Carolyn Whitworth Brittain, Annie Stith-Willis, Ann Williams, Anne P. Bryant and Bob and Wilma Andrews. I also want to acknowledge the staff of the YardBird Center for their support. Accordingly, I would like to thank Mark Ackerman, Linda Ackerman, Barb Skidmore, Kathy Louthan, Travis Anthony, "Reacher" and "Lucy."

As usual, The History Press was very kind and helpful. I would like to acknowledge the encouragement, expertise and support of J. Banks Smither, Darcy Mahan, Meredith Riddick, Karmen Cook and Katie Parry.

Finally, I would like to thank the students at Virginia Commonwealth University who took my course on the *Titanic*. Together, we shared some very emotional moments as "the great ship went down."

Introduction

The Sinking of the Titanic *is an appalling catastrophe, in the contemplation of which any words that can be uttered are as futile as in the presence of the awful majesty of the Angel of Death.*
—Jay Henry Mowbray

In the fall of 1912, a door-to-door salesman visited my great-grandparents' florist on Mechanicsville Turnpike in Richmond, Virginia. This salesman was selling a book entitled *Sinking of the Titanic* by Jay Henry Mowbray. On the title page is this statement: "Sinking of the *Titanic:* Most appalling ocean horror with graphic descriptions of hundreds swept to eternity beneath the waves; panic stricken multitude facing sure death; and thrilling stories of this most overwhelming catastrophe." My great-grandmother purchased the book for one dollar. Sometime later, she wrote her name, Mrs. Chas. R. Steinbach, on the front page.

This book, based on newspaper articles and firsthand accounts, tells the tragic—if not completely accurate—story of that night in 1912 when the lights of a great ocean liner were extinguished by the cold Atlantic Ocean and dead human beings were left to float on the surface among the icebergs and deck chairs. Based on the worn cover and coffee-stained pages, my great-grandmother must have read the book many times. The first words she would have read in the book are as follows: "We are as near Heaven by sea as by land." The book ends with these words: "The *Titanic* was expected to make a record on her maiden voyage. She made one unapproached in ocean annals; one which, it is hoped, may long stand unparalleled."

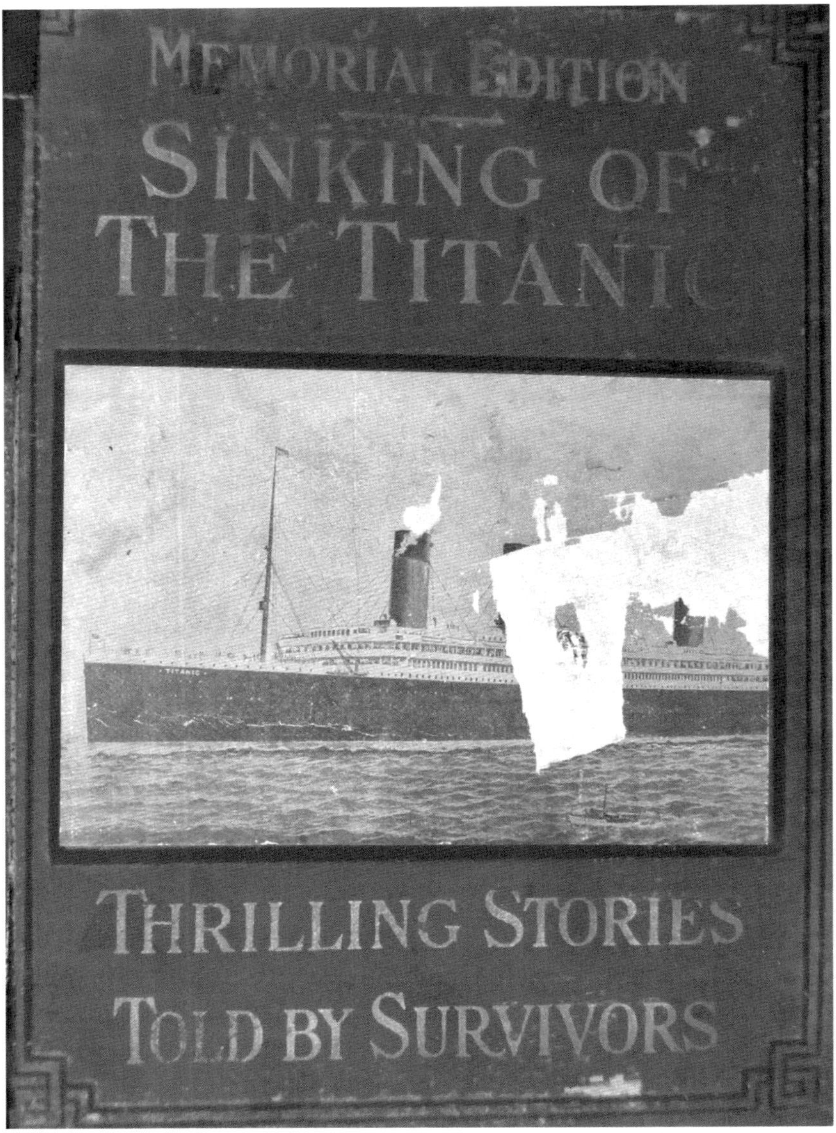

Sinking of the Titanic, the book my great-grandmother bought. *Author's collection.*

Carrie Steinbach, like many Richmonders, was captivated by the sinking of the RMS *Titanic* and the tragic loss of so many lives. Although over one hundred years have passed since the night the "great ship went down," its story is timeless. "*Titanic*" remains one of the most recognizable words in the English language and still reminds people of the horrible tragedy and the unnecessary loss of life on a star-spangled, crystal-clear Sunday night in April 1912.

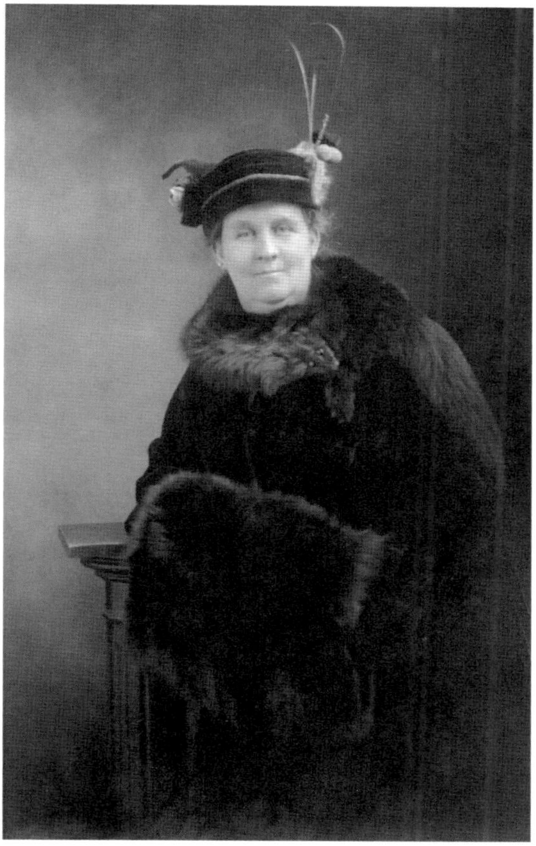

Carrie Lee Steinbach, who bought the *Titanic book*. *Author's collection.*

I was given my great-grandmother's book as a young boy, and I spent many hours looking at the artist's pictures of the sinking ship. These horrific images captured my imagination. When I learned to read, I read the gripping accounts of those who faced death when the *Titanic* struck an iceberg and there were not enough lifeboats to save everyone on board from death in the North Atlantic. Many times I have wondered how I would have acted if I had been on this ship and realized that I would have drowned for lack of lifeboats. It is a haunting thought. I still think about it!

On April 15, 1912, Richmonders learned from a brief article on the front page of the *Times Dispatch* that the *Titanic* had struck an iceberg. For the next several weeks, the daily newspapers were devoted to the story of the ocean liner and everything associated with it. Heroes and villains emerged as stories about the sinking of the great ship were reported.

This book begins with the story of the *Titanic*'s voyage to disaster and concludes with daily articles from the Richmond newspapers that will enable the reader to relive the event as Richmonders did in 1912.

WALTER S. GRIGGS JR.
Henrico, Virginia

Chapter 1

Birth of an Iceberg

The ice was here, the ice was there,
The ice was all around:
It crashed and growled, and roared and howled,
Like noises in a swound!
—Samuel Tayler Coleridge, "Rime of the Ancient Mariner"

Over ten thousand years ago, snow fell on an island now called Greenland. The snow would have only been noticed by wandering polar bears, perhaps a stalwart musk ox or other Arctic wildlife. It fell at a time when wooly mammoths and saber-toothed tigers were passing into extinction, humans were emerging from their caves, Stonehenge was being built and Native Americans lived in a land that they called Turtle Island but would be called Virginia when the English settlers arrived at Jamestown.

When the snow started to accumulate, it began forming a massive glacier, which, over thousands of years, started moving slowly toward the sea. Meanwhile, Greenland was being populated by the Vikings, led by Erick the Red, who led his followers from Iceland in their ferocious-looking "dragon ships." It was Erick the Red who named the large island Greenland since he thought an attractive name might attract settlers to the island. These early settlers were tough. King Hardradi, who was associated with the Vikings, wrote, "I kill without compunction and remember all of my killings." In such a hostile environment, you had to be a tough person.

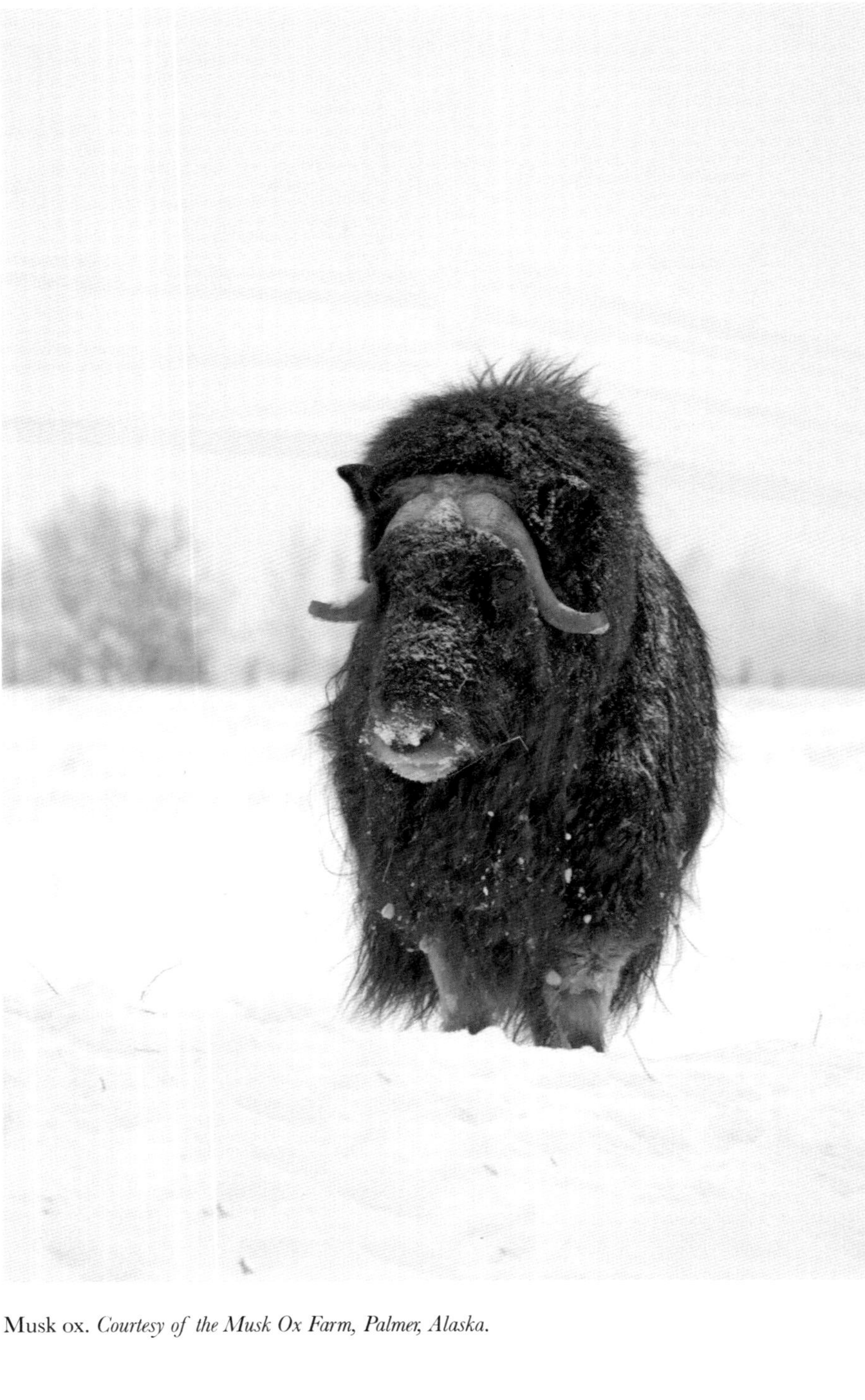

Musk ox. *Courtesy of the Musk Ox Farm, Palmer, Alaska.*

While Greenland became home to some hardy souls over many decades, the glacier that was formed from the ancient snowfall continued to move slowly toward the sea. Finally, in early 1912, the glacier reached the waters surrounding Greenland, broke free and crashed into the sea, disturbing narwhals and killer whales and scaring the auks and kittiwakes. The birth of an iceberg is known as calving, and the newly formed mountain of ice floated into the Atlantic Ocean. The Vikings believed that these floating ice mountains looked like the fortresses of their gods Odin and Thor. They called these floating mountains "icebergs," which means mountains of ice. The iceberg that was born, when it cracked loose from the glacier with a great noise and fell into the sea, was destined to melt in the warm waters of the South Atlantic—but not before it destroyed the *Titanic* on her maiden voyage.

As it floated south, only one-tenth of its volume was above water; the rest of it lurked unseen under the water. Soon "tip of the iceberg" entered the lexicon of the English language both as a descriptive term and as a warning for shipping that was not always heeded. This iceberg that was created in the land of the polar bears would soon become known, and remain known, throughout the world as the iceberg that sank the RMS *Titanic*.

The ocean liner *Titanic* was built thousands of years after the Greenland snowfall evolved into an iceberg. It was the largest moving object ever made by man and was the pride of a nation. There were even those who thought it to be unsinkable. The collision of the ancient works of nature and the modern works of man was destined to send over 1,500 souls to eternity.

Richmonders were familiar with Greenland and its icebergs. In 1902, an article appeared in the *Richmond Dispatch* suggesting that the United States should annex Greenland. Although the article was basically good-natured humor, the writer did mention icebergs as coming from Greenland. He commented, "In the ocean roundabout, the wary halibut tempts the fisherman, and the lone leviathan blows his nose among the echoing icebergs." The author then concluded that the United States did not need any "blubbering, gulping children" from Greenland. It was also pointed out that Greenland lacked heat and running water. It did not seem an attractive land for annexation.

In addition to comments about Greenland, there were frequent articles about icebergs in the Richmond newspapers. Icebergs were a hazard to ocean navigation and were frequently struck by ships. When there was such a collision, it was reported as front-page news—and there were plenty of front-page stories about icebergs.

Indeed, Richmond newspapers as far back as 1854 carried stories of ships striking icebergs under a variety of circumstances. For example, the British bark *Britton* struck an iceberg in a dense fog and was sunk. The crew was saved. In 1859, the Richmond newspapers carried this story about the steamship *Edinburg*: "The iceberg was first discovered directly ahead of the ship. The helm was put hard a port, and she passed without touching the part above water; but struck under water near the port bow and stove in one of the forward plates." This accident was similar to what would happen to the *Titanic* over fifty years later.

The Canadian ship *Harworth* hit an iceberg that the lookout thought was a low-hanging cloud. It was a clear and starlit night. The *Titanic* hit an iceberg on a clear and starlit night. The *Sala*, a German ship, struck an iceberg but was able to make port with only her paint scratched. The captain reported that the ship was moving very slowly, and that probably saved her. The *Titanic* was plowing through the ocean at top speed when she struck an iceberg. This accident was soon followed by news of the *Norman*. Richmonders learned that "during a dense fog, she had a slight collision with an iceberg which the ship's captain thought would have been serious had it not been for her double screws [propellers] which enabled the ship to try to swing around the iceberg." Although the ship struck the iceberg, there was little damage. The *Titanic* tried a similar course correction with disastrous results.

Not so fortunate was the *Rose Henry*, a fishing schooner that struck an iceberg and sunk within ten minutes. Fortunately, another fishing vessel was nearby and was able to save some crew members, but twelve men lost their lives. Those who were saved had managed to crawl onto the iceberg to wait for a rescue vessel.

On June 6, 1894, some Richmonders were on board the Anchor Line steamer *Ethiopia* on a voyage from New York to Glasgow. A dense fog made visibility difficult, and the ship crashed into an iceberg off the coast of Newfoundland. A passenger from Richmond wrote: "The iceberg was very near the ship when first seen by the captain who was on the bridge of the ship. The engines were immediately reversed, which slackened the speed, and when the collision occurred the ship was nearly stopped." The hull was pierced, but the crew was able to stop the leak using some timber and sails. The ship continued on to Glasgow, where it arrived safely. The newspaper did not state who from Richmond wrote the letter, but the Richmonders on board were James F. Netherland, Alice and Emma Netherland, Mrs. Dr. William E. Hatcher and O.L. Hatcher. Since a Richmonder wrote about the collision at sea, this accident attracted the attention of a lot of people in the city.

In those days of very primitive communication, a note in a bottle told the story of one lost ship. The bottle and its note were found on the Hebrides Island. The note, written in pencil, was as follows: "September, 1893. Sinking mid-Atlantic *Hornshead.* Collision Iceberg. (signed) Mate" The ship had sailed from Hampton Roads, Virginia, and the note told its fate. Until the bottle was found, no one knew what had happened to the ship.

A year before the *Titanic* tragedy, the liner *Columbia* struck an iceberg. The *Columbia* had stopped when an iceberg floated into it. The ship was saved, and the holes were covered with canvas. Fortunately, all of the damage was above the waterline. The damage to the ship was clearly visible when she arrived in New York City. Because of the many published stories in the Richmond newspapers, Richmonders were well aware of the dangers associated with encountering icebergs in the North Atlantic.

Richmonders not only read about icebergs; they might also have seen them since it was not unknown for icebergs to appear off the Virginia coast. In the late 1890s, Captain Hudson of the British steamer *Gulf of Taranto* reported an iceberg in the Chesapeake Bay. This was in addition to the report of icebergs being observed off Cape Hatteras. There were even claims that they had been observed off the coast of Norfolk, Virginia. Perhaps these local sightings and collisions with ships encouraged many Richmonders to attend a speech on icebergs by Dr. Jacob Michaux at the Richmond Young Men's Christian Association. Reportedly, the speech was well attended and very interesting.

A concerned citizen who might have attended the speech wrote, "Many perfectly good ships were leaving port never to be heard from again. With no means to communicate a distress call, both ship and crew slipped into a watery grave never to be found." The author urged that the "United States send navy ships to patrol the area [where icebergs were known to drift] and put some sort of lights on them to warn ships that an iceberg was in the shipping lanes." It was even suggested that these navy ships on "ice police duty" might gain some practical experience by torpedoing the icebergs. In addition to torpedoing icebergs, a unique device was installed on the steamship *St. Paul.* The ship had an iron cage placed over her bow with a giant searchlight mounted on it. The idea was that seamen would use the searchlight to locate icebergs. In another article read by many Richmonders, it was suggested that some means might be discovered to protect ships "within the next century as science goes on its progressive way." Although no one invented a practical way to destroy icebergs, Guglielmo Marconi provided a way for ships to communicate a distress signal if they should be in danger of sinking.

Marconi had worked to find a way to communicate across the Atlantic Ocean in order to compete with the transatlantic telegraph cables. Success was achieved on December 17, 1902, when the first wireless message crossed the Atlantic. On January 18, 1903, a wireless message was exchanged between President Theodore Roosevelt of the United States and King Edward VII of England. Before long, ships were using wireless to send messages from passengers and to send distress signals. The work of this one man would be responsible for saving the passengers and crew of the *Titanic* and many other ships.

The *Times Dispatch* reported that the steamer *St. Cuthbert* caught fire and was saved by a wireless message that enabled another ship to come to her aid. Richmonders read about this and heard lectures at the Richmond YMCA about Marconi and his new wireless technology. Truly, Richmonders were very interested in this new means of communication and would become much more interested when the wireless operator on the *Titanic* tapped out SOS.

By 1912, Richmonders were well aware of the dangers of icebergs and the invention of the wireless. What Richmonders did not know was that all prior collisions with icebergs would pale in comparison to the one that would occur on April 14, 1912.

Chapter 2

The Hymn

Nearer, My God, to Thee, Nearer to Thee!
E'en though it be a cross that raiseth me;
Still all my songs shall be,
Nearer, My God, to Thee.
Nearer to Thee!
—*Sarah Flower Adams*

One of the reasons that interest in the *Titanic* has continued for over one hundred years is the mystery surrounding some events associated with the sinking of the ship. One of these mysteries concerns the last composition that the musicians played as the "great ship went down." Current scholarship suggests that the popular songs of the day were played when the *Titanic* first hit the iceberg. These selections included the following: "Oh, You Beautiful Doll," "Alexander's Ragtime Band," "Shine on Harvest Moon," "Glow Worm" and "Waiting for the Robert E. Lee." But when all hope was lost, tradition suggests that the musicians played "Nearer, My God, to Thee."

"Nearer, My God, to Thee" was written by Sarah Flower Adams, who was born in 1805 at High Street, Old Harlow, Essex, England. Raised by their father, Sarah and her sister Elizabeth attended the Unitarian Church, and Sarah became a Unitarian. On September 24, 1834, Sarah married William Adams, a civil engineer.

Her biographer, H.W. Stephenson, believed that her faith journey led Sarah not to accept dogma blindly; rather, "she built up her own faith with

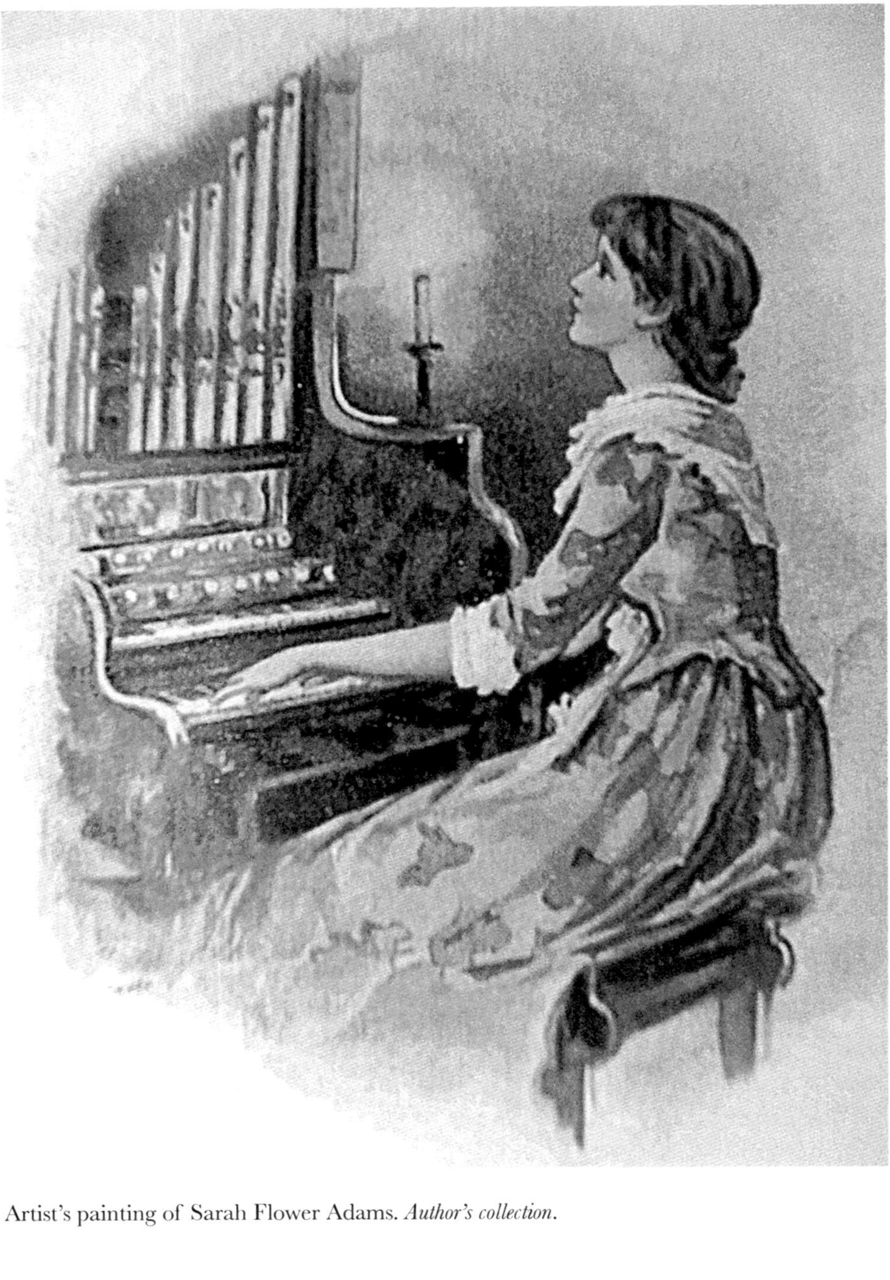

Artist's painting of Sarah Flower Adams. *Author's collection.*

such aid as she might derive from the spiritual atmosphere and doctrinal media with which she was most intimately in contact." Sarah was a very talented woman who, in addition to her spiritual quest, followed several other pursuits. She was a noted actress who once played Lady Macbeth at the Little Richmond Theater in England. She was also a prolific writer of poems and essays.

There are several stories about why Sarah Adams wrote "Nearer, My God, to Thee." One story involved a Unitarian minister, the Reverend William Johnson Fox of London's South Place Unitarian Church. He commented to Sarah Adams that he could not find a hymn to fit his Sunday's sermon based on the text from Genesis 28:11–12. The verses told the story of Jacob dreaming that there was a ladder to heaven and that angels were ascending and descending on it. Perhaps Sarah saw the ladder as a way to get nearer to God.

Another story was that Reverend Fox was writing a hymnal and asked Sarah Adams to write some hymns for it. One of the hymns selected for inclusion in the hymn book was "Nearer, My God, to Thee."

Other accounts suggest that the hymn was written while Sarah was going through a mental and spiritual struggle. She had known grief throughout her life and was not in good health. Perhaps coming out of a time of despair, she felt she had become "Nearer, My God, to Thee."

"Nearer, My God, to Thee" was first published in the hymnal *Hymns and Anthems* in 1841. It was published in the United States in 1856 in the hymnal *Sabbath Hymns and Tune Book*. Tragically, Sarah Adams died at the age of forty-three before she knew how gratefully the world would receive her hymn—a hymn that gave comfort to many people in difficult circumstances.

Perhaps one of the first times that Richmonders would have learned of the hymn was when it was played by a Confederate band following Pickett's disastrous charge at Gettysburg, Pennsylvania, on July 3, 1863. But it was also associated with many other events known to Richmonders.

President William McKinley, while dying of an assassin's bullet, repeated the phrase "Nearer, My God, to Thee." This hymn was sung at a memorial service for him held at the state capitol building in Richmond. It was also sung at his memorial services at Centenary Methodist Church and at Central Methodist Church, both located in Richmond.

In England, the hymn was played at the funeral of England's King Edward VII in 1910 by the Salvation Army band. The *Times Dispatch* reported that the band knelt, the leader led them in prayer and then they played "Nearer, My God, to Thee." Increasingly, this hymn was played at funerals on both sides of the Atlantic.

In 1883, it was sung at a meeting of the Woman's Christian Temperance Union Convention in Richmond at Seventh Street Christian Church. The convention and the hymn received extensive coverage in the local newspapers.

In 1889, the South Fork Dam failed, causing twenty million tons of water to cascade into Johnstown, Pennsylvania. The catastrophic flood claimed the lives of over 2,200 people. Survivors recalled that a woman who could not be rescued started singing "Nearer, My God, to Thee." Her voice was heard until the surging waters swept her into eternity.

In 1903, there was an explosion in one of the forward gun turrets on board the American battleship USS *Massachusetts*. The explosion killed eight sailors. At a funeral service held on board the ship, the ship's chaplain asked the officers and men to sing "Nearer, My God, to Thee."

Another sea disaster associated with the hymn occurred in 1906 when the SS *Valencia*, a small ocean liner, struck a reef off the southwest coast of Vancouver Island in the Pacific Ocean. One survivor wrote, "Screams of women and children mingled in an awful chorus with the shrieking of the wind, the dash of rain, and the roar of the breakers. Because of the fierce storm, rescue vessels had great difficulty reaching the sinking ship. It was a pitiful sight to see frail women, wearing only night dresses with bare feet holding to the freezing ratlines, trying to shield children in their arms from the wind and rain."

Although the exact number of those lost in this disaster is unknown, it was between 150 and 200. What is so amazing is that the "women, seemingly looking death in the face, were able, in the fog and flying spray, to sing 'Nearer, My God, to Thee.'" Another account suggested that both the crew and the women were singing the hymn together. Once again, it was Sarah Adams's hymn that was sung when death seemed imminent. Details of this tragedy were published several times in the Richmond newspapers.

In March 1912, a month before the *Titanic* sank, there was a meditation in the *Times Dispatch* in which the words of "Nearer, My God, to Thee" were printed. It was suggested by the writer that the words of this hymn should be repeated regularly as a prayer. He even suggested that it was the only prayer people would ever need. The hymn was also the one that was played at the funerals of members of England's Amalgamated Musicians' Union.

And in England, a young violinist whose career would lead him to play on ocean liners learned to play the hymn. His name was Wallace Hartley. In April 1912, he boarded a ship with his violin to lead the musicians on the maiden voyage of the newest ocean liner in the White Star's fleet. As he walked up the gangplank, the word "*Titanic*" could be seen on her freshly painted bow.

Chapter 3

"They Built the Ship *Titanic*"

Oh, they built the ship Titanic, *to sail the ocean blue*
And they thought they had a ship that the water wouldn't go through
But the good Lord raised His hand, said the ship would never land
It was sad when the great ship went down.
—*author unknown*

King Edward VII was the king of England in 1907, and his reign was known as the Edwardian Age. During his reign, Great Britain was the most powerful nation on earth. The Union Jack was flying proudly over many nations. It was a time of peace and plenty with no depressions and widespread prosperity. These conditions resulted in some very wealthy people who constituted the upper class at a time when Great Britain had a rigid class system and a rigid social protocol.

The upper class was sometimes described as a leisure class whose members lived in beautiful homes, held lucrative positions and were fashionable in their dress. Women in this era wore corsets, long dresses and tunics. For travel, a frequent choice was a tailored suit with matching jacket and skirt. Women frequently changed their attire five times a day to meet different social occasions. Men dressed in impeccable fashion, usually wearing sack coats, three-piece suits and ankle-length trousers with cuffs. Many wealthy families employed servants to attend to their personal needs. Some of the jobs performed by servants included chauffer, personal maid, governess, personal cook and nursemaid. Indeed, these servants were frequently taken on trips to take care of luggage and other family needs. Because of their wealth, the upper class had no difficulty in spending their money on luxury travel on ships to North America or to any other place they might want to go. It was in this age, and for this age, that the *Titanic* was built.

In the summer of 1907, J. Bruce Ismay, the chairman of the White Star Line, met with Lord Pirrie, chairman of the Harland and Wolff shipbuilders of Belfast, Ireland, at Lord Pirrie's London residence, Devonshire House (now the Spanish embassy). The two men and their companies had maintained a close business relationship. The White Star Line had had many contracts with Harland and Wolff to build ships. Following a meal with their wives, these two men discussed a problem and how to solve it. The issue was how the White Star Line could successfully compete with the RMS *Lusitania* and the RMS *Mauretania*, the two new ships of arch rival Cunard Line, on the North Atlantic run from England to North America. These two new Cunard liners were designed to be the fastest on the North Atlantic run and became a major competitor of the White Star Line. The existing White Star liners, the RMS *Teutonic*, the RMS *Oceanic* and the RMS *Adriatic*, were not fast enough to compete successfully with the Cunard ships. The White Star Line could try to build even faster ships, but maybe there was another option.

Richmonders were familiar with both of the two new Cunard liners. The *Times Dispatch* had a front-page picture of the *Lusitania* on September 13, 1907, the day she arrived in New York Harbor. It was further reported that she almost beat the transatlantic record without even operating under full power. The *Times Dispatch* also gave front-page coverage to the RMS *Mauretania* when she arrived in New York after completing her voyage from England to New York City on November 2, 1907. Since so much publicity had been given to the *Lusitania*, much less publicity was given to the *Mauretania*. However, the Richmond newspapers revealed that she was faster than the *Lusitania*, but the newspaper also reported that the Cunard Line did not want the public to know this. It was reported as follows: "The *Lusitania* is already outclassed. Every effort is being made by the Cunard Line to postpone publicity, but it has been completely established that her younger sister, the *Mauretania*, is almost two knots faster than the *Lusitania*." The Cunard Line became known for the speed of its ships. In the years ahead, the *Mauretania* would become a legend for her long service while the *Lusitania* would be sunk by a German U-boat with the loss of many lives. The sinking of this ship was a primary reason that the United States entered World War I.

Although Cunard was known for fast ships, Ismay and Pirrie, at their meeting amid floating cigar smoke, coffee cups and maybe brandy, made a critical decision. They had a different idea. They proposed to build ships that were both comfortable and safe but would not challenge the Cunard liners for speed. It was believed that passengers would not mind a few extra hours at sea if they could enjoy them in comfort and luxury that surpassed that of any other ocean liner. And since speed was not the goal, the ship would be quieter and have less engine vibrations to annoy the passengers. In the final analysis, the White Star Line chose luxury over speed.

As part of the commitment to make the trip as comfortable as possible, the staterooms and the saloon would be placed amidships to avoid the sounds of the engines. Perhaps Harland and Wolff had learned from the mistakes of the German-built *Deutschland*, whose engines vibrated so badly that she was known as a "cocktail shake." Indeed, the White Star Line had a firm commitment to "excellence" in all aspects of shipbuilding and passenger comfort.

Although the *Titanic* is best remembered for its opulent first-class accommodations, its second-class accommodations were equal to first class on many ships. Even the lowest grade of accommodation was given consideration. Traditionally called steerage or the "glory hole" because it was close to the engines where there was more noise, it was now called third class, and the accommodations were superior to similar accommodations on other ocean liners. It was in third class that those who were seeking a new life in America were traveling.

Providing the funding for this massive undertaking was J.P. Morgan, an American financier and the founding owner of the International Mercantile Marine Company, which was the owner of the White Star Line. Like Great Britain's upper class, there was great wealth in the hands of some Americans, like Morgan, during what has been termed the "Gilded Age" in the United States.

The decision to build such large ships for the White Star Line faced a major challenge. There were no shipyards big enough to construct these large ships; therefore, Harland and Wolff built two specially strengthened shipways known as No. 2 and No. 3 at the Belfast Ship Yard of Harland and Wolff. And across the Atlantic, the City of New York extended the White Star Line piers in New York Harbor to accommodate these large ships. Because of his influence, J.P. Morgan was able to have these piers extended by the City of New York into the North River with no cost to the White Star Line.

Following subsequent discussions, three sister ships were planned for the White Star Line. With three ships, the White Star Line would be able to offer weekly service between England and North America. This would be accomplished by having one ship going east, one ship going west and one ship being resupplied and prepared for the next voyage. An agreement was signed on July 31, 1908, to build the first two ships. The RMS *Olympic* was the first one to be placed under construction at the Harland and Wolff shipyard on Queen's Island, Belfast, Ireland.

Following the start of the construction of the *Olympic*, the *Titanic*'s keel was laid on March 31, 1909. Its name was derived from Greek mythology about a legendary race of people known as Titans, which means something very large. Such powerful names were not considered a good omen since they were seen to challenge Providence. This concern began with the seamen during the Elizabethan era. The names were probably selected by the White Star Line to emphasize the size of the ships when compared with their Cunard rivals. There is another aspect of the names that is of interest: the names of all White Star Line ships ended with the suffix "ic," and all Cunard Line ships ended with the suffix "ia."

During construction, the ship to be named *Titanic* was simply known as Hull No. 401. The final ship in the class was, according to some authorities, to be named the *Gigantic*, but this name was changed to the *Britannic* following the loss of the *Titanic*. The *Britannic* entered service in 1915 as a hospital ship during World War I and was sunk either by a torpedo or a mine. It is ironic that all of these ships were built to go from England to New York, but only the *Olympic* ever made the trip successfully. The *Titanic* was a casualty of nature and the *Britannic* a casualty of war.

Thomas Andrews, who was the head of the design department of Harland and Wolff, was one of the primary overseers of the construction of the *Titanic*. During this process, he was constantly checking on everything. He knew the *Titanic* better than anyone else and was highly regarded by both the management and the workers for his skill, his commitment to excellence and his concern for the shipbuilders.

At one point, Andrews suggested that the *Titanic* should have more lifeboats, along with other additional safety devices. Unfortunately, his suggestion was not implemented. The British Board of Trade had not changed its lifeboat regulations since 1894; consequently, no adjustment was made for the large liners that were currently under construction or in use. Using the formulas in the existing regulations, the *Titanic* was required to carry lifeboats for only 962 people when she had an actual capacity of 3,547 people. This meant that she had lifeboats for about one-third of those on board. Since the *Titanic* sailed on her maiden voyage with many vacant staterooms, she had enough lifeboats for about 53 percent of those who were actually on board the night she struck the iceberg. Legally, the *Titanic* was in compliance with regard to the number of lifeboats; in fact, she had more than were required—but still not enough.

Alexander Carlisle, who supervised the construction of the *Titanic*, also suggested that more lifeboats should be carried on the ship. He knew that the *Titanic* was capable of carrying enough lifeboats for all of the passengers. However, additional lifeboats were seen as cluttering the decks, spoiling the beauty of the ship, and would take up space that could be used to provide more deck space for the passengers to enjoy. Indeed, it had been reported that less than thirty minutes were spent on the lifeboat proposals, but many hours were spent discussing décor. It could be concluded that a fashionable ship was more important than a safe ship.

There was an additional line of reasoning concerning lifeboats. At the time the *Titanic* was built, it was felt that another ship would always be nearby in case of an emergency and the lifeboats were only to be used to ferry passengers between two ships. Since this enabled the lifeboats to be used over and over again, it was felt that a lifeboat seat for every passenger was not needed. This idea, however, was fallacious, and the moral requirement to provide a lifeboat seat for all passengers was completely ignored. In essence, the law had not kept up with the new trends in shipbuilding.

From the perspective of history, it seems incomprehensible that a ship would set sail with lifeboats for only a fraction of the people on board. The fact that this argument for more lifeboats was lost, based on both law and appearance, probably cost the lives of over one thousand people on a cold April night. Sometimes a decision made at one point in time comes back to haunt the decision makers at a much later date. One casualty of this decision was Thomas Andrews.

The *Titanic* was ready for launching on May 31, 1911, from slip number 3, which incorporated some of the design features of the shipyard at Newport News, Virginia. Prior to launching, twenty-two tons of tallow and soap were spread on the shipway to aid the ship's slide into the water. In front of the ship there was this sign: "White Star; Royal Mail Steamer, *Titanic*."

At 12:05 p.m., a red rocket was fired into the air over Belfast from the Harland and Wolff Shipyard to warn other crafts that a launch was imminent and for other ships to stay clear. At 12:10 p.m., another rocket arched into the sky to notify everyone a launch would take place in five minutes, and at 12:14 p.m., another rocket signaled the launch. Then, more than 100,000 people screamed, "There she goes" as the largest man-made floating object

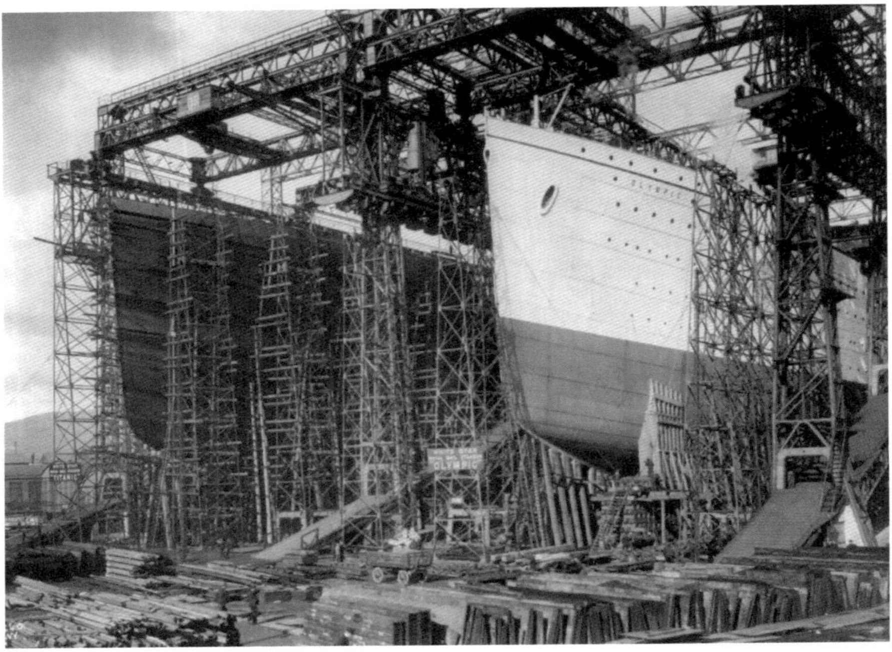

Titanic under construction at Belfast. *Courtesy of Wikimedia Commons.*

ever built slid into the water. The launch took only sixty-two seconds. Once in the water, the *Titanic* was towed to a graving dock, where she would be "fitted out" for her ocean debut. Her signal flags proclaimed, "Good Luck."

During the launch, a shipyard worker commented about the lack of a formal ceremony or christening. He quipped, "They just builds 'er and shoves 'er in." In contrast, the Cunard Line always had a formal christening of its ships. Over three thousand workmen had built the *Titanic*. Eight died, and 246 injuries were recorded with 28 of them being classified as serious. Little regard was given to the safety of those working on ships, including the *Titanic*. Tossing and catching red-hot rivets, working on high scaffolding and walking on small boards high in the air over metal plates was dangerous work that caused many injuries. In fact, one shipyard worker was crushed to death when the *Titanic* was launched.

The sheer magnitude of the new ship was recorded by a Belfast resident in the following article:

> *For months and months in that monstrous iron enclosure there was nothing that had the faintest likeness to a ship; only something that might have*

> *been the iron scaffolding for the nave of half-a-dozen cathedrals end to end…at last the skeleton within the scaffold began to take shape at the sight of which men held their breaths. It was the shape of a ship, a ship so monstrous and unthinkable that it towered there over the buildings and dwarfed the very mountains by the water—a rudder as big as a giant elm tree bearing off propellers the size of windmills—everything was on a nightmare scale…and when the moment came, the water she was to conquer should thrust her finally from earth.*

Richmonders knew of the launch of the *Titanic*. The *Times Dispatch* of June 1, 1911, carried this story: "The White Star Liner *Titanic* was launched in the River Laffan in Belfast, Ireland." The newspaper further reported that "the *Titanic* would enter the Southampton–New York Service later in the year." The *Olympic* and *Titanic* were described as "sea monsters." In addition to the news of the launch, there were numerous advertisements in the Richmond newspapers concerning ocean travel on these and other ocean liners.

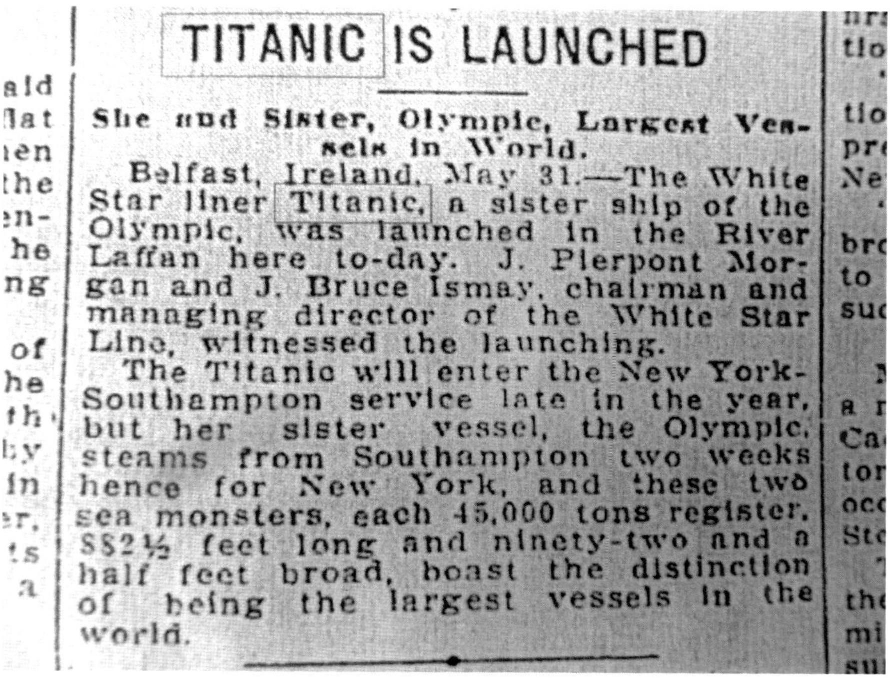

TITANIC IS LAUNCHED

She and Sister, Olympic, Largest Vessels in World.

Belfast, Ireland, May 31.—The White Star liner Titanic, a sister ship of the Olympic, was launched in the River Laffan here to-day. J. Pierpont Morgan and J. Bruce Ismay, chairman and managing director of the White Star Line, witnessed the launching.

The Titanic will enter the New York-Southampton service late in the year, but her sister vessel, the Olympic, steams from Southampton two weeks hence for New York, and these two sea monsters, each 45,000 tons register, 882½ feet long and ninety-two and a half feet broad, boast the distinction of being the largest vessels in the world.

Story in the *Times Dispatch* about the launching of the *Titanic*. *Author's collection.*

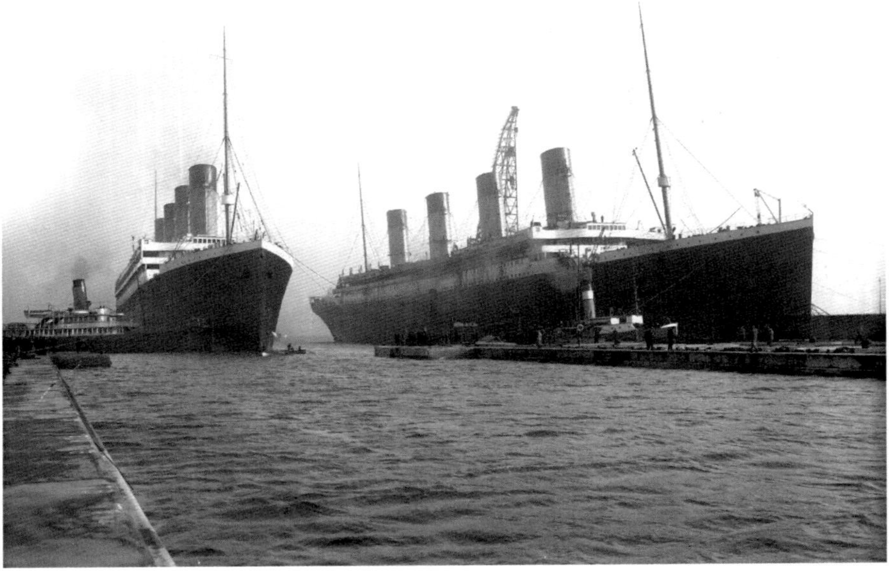

Titanic and *Olympic* together at Belfast. Possibly the only picture of the two sister ships together. *Courtesy of Wikimedia Commons.*

For example, there was a large advertisement promoting White Star Line Transatlantic Service. Under a picture of a White Star ship was this comment: "White Star steamers *Olympic* and *Titanic* largest and finest vessels in the world. Information on securing tickets is available from Mr. Bowman, Southern Steamship and Tourist Agent, 708 East Main Street, Richmond, Virginia, or phone Madison 5154." For purposes of marketing, the White Star Line let the public know that the *Olympic* and *Titanic* were 120 feet longer and twelve tons larger than their Cunard rivals.

The Richmond newspaper then carried another story that the White Star Line was planning to build a new ocean liner that would be just fewer than one thousand feet in length and would make these newly planned, larger ships even larger than the ones being completed. It could be concluded that size and comfort would be the hallmark of the ships crossing the Atlantic under the pennant of the White Star Line.

Shortly after the *Titanic* was launched, the *Olympic* arrived in New York following her maiden voyage. The *Times Dispatch* reported on its front page that "twelve stout tugboats strained and pulled on the White Star Liner to its pier." The *Olympic* made an average speed of 21.17 knots on her maiden

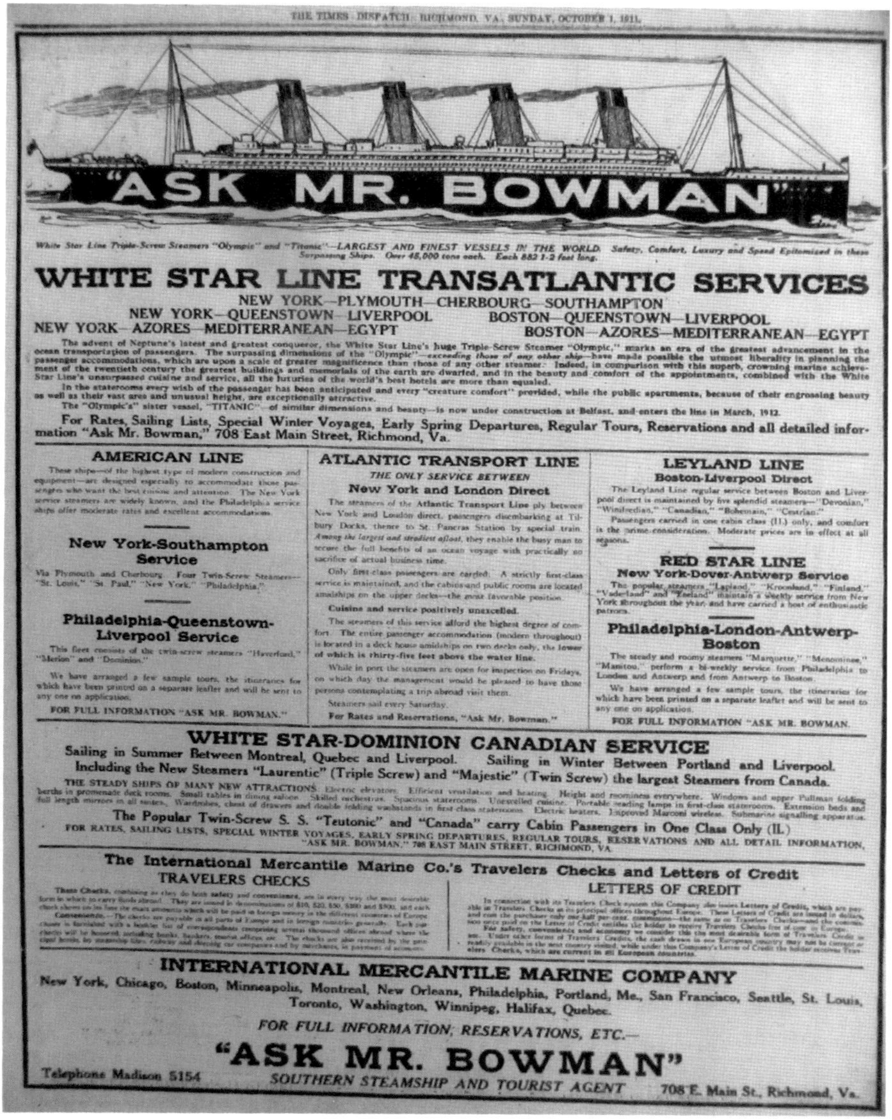

Newspaper advertisement for travel on the *Titanic*. *Author's collection.*

run, crossing the Atlantic in five days, sixteen hours and forty-two minutes. It was also reported that she was "nearly 100 feet longer than any other ship on the transatlantic run." Pictures showed that *Olympic* was taller than the great pyramid and longer than the United States Capitol building.

The *Titanic* was soon ready to cross the Atlantic in the wake of the *Olympic*. The White Star Line released the following information about the ship: "The *Titanic* was 882 feet 9 inches long, its beam was 92 feet; its gross tonnage was 46,328 tons; she had three propellers; two triple-expansion steam engines; one low pressure Parsons Turbine; 25 double-ended and four single-ended Scotch type boilers; 159 coal burning furnaces; and could reach a top speed of 23 knots. She had ten decks and four funnels. The *Titanic's* hull was made of overlapping steel plates fastened by over 3 million rivets, and 200 miles of electric cable ran through the ship. The hull was built with a double bottom, and for safety reasons, she was divided into sixteen watertight compartments." For some reason, the bulkheads creating the watertight compartments did not go up high enough, which would prove a fatal flaw. If the ship started to sink by the bow, the watertight doors would hold the water in a compartment, but as the angle of the dive increased, the water would fill up one compartment and then spill over the top of the next bulkhead to fill another and another. Eventually, sufficient compartments would fill and the ship would sink. The *Titanic* could stay afloat with any two of the middle compartments or four of the first five compartments flooded. These watertight compartments were built on the assumption that the worst collision would only breach two of them. It was a fatal assumption.

Although the builders never made the claim, there was a common notion that the *Titanic* was unsinkable. Captain Edward J. Smith, who would command the ship, once commented, "I cannot imagine any condition which would cause a ship to founder. I cannot conceive of any vital disaster happening…Modern ship building has gone beyond that." Indeed, Philip A.S. Franklin, the vice-president of the International Mercantile Marine, believed the *Titanic* was unsinkable. History would prove otherwise. On February 3, 1912, the ship was moved to a dry dock to be completed. While being fitted out, she was assigned the wireless call sign MGY.

On April 2, 1912, at 6:00 a.m., the *Titanic* was taken out for her sea trials. In command was Captain Edward J. Smith, the popular captain of the White Star Line who was making his final transatlantic crossing before he retired. In his career, he had commanded seventeen White Star ocean liners. The sea trials lasted twelve hours and included various maneuvers such as stopping and turning and numerous other maneuvers that the ship might have to make as she sailed across the Atlantic. Following the tests, the *Titanic* was awarded a "Certificate of Seaworthiness" and thus became the newest member of the White Star Line.

Prior to her departure from Belfast, W.J. Nolan, who had worked on the *Titanic*, witnessed an unsettling event. He observed that a portion of the ship was covered with birds. Birds were coming and going every second. Indeed, some birds landed on the port side, walked across the ship and took flight off the starboard side. While not on the ship, they circled it, producing a creepy noise. Such behavior by birds was a sign of bad luck for seamen. A sailor said, "This means something terrible is going to happen to us before this voyage is over." These birds were probably storm petrels. Early sailors called them "Mother Carey's chickens" because they were thought to warn of oncoming storms. The name is based on a corruption of "Mater Cara," a name for the Virgin Mary. This odd and unsettling occurrence was kept a secret by those who observed it for fear of upsetting the crew.

Another concern was that the crew used playing cards with the number 999 on them. When inverted, these numbers became 666 or the "Mark of the Beast" in the biblical book of Revelations. If people were looking for bad omens, there were plenty to be found.

The *Titanic* was now ready to sail, an iceberg was floating south and the hymn "Nearer, My God, to Thee" had been written. In a matter of days, the ship, the iceberg and the hymn would become part of one of the world's greatest tragedies. It was only a matter of time…only a matter of time.

Chapter 4
Underway

A ship rode forth on the Noonday tide
Rode forth to the open sea
And high sun shone on the good ship's side
And all seemed gladness and hope, and pride
For the gallant sight she was.
—Father Frank Browne, SJ

Having received the proper certificate, tugboats guided the *Titanic* into the channel and then the engine order telegraph was pushed to the desired speed. The *Titanic* left her birthplace in Belfast at 8:00 p.m. on April 2 and set sail for the port at Southampton, England. Reaching speeds of around eighteen knots, she arrived after midnight on April 3, 1912. The *Titanic* had traveled almost six hundred miles without any incident and was docked at berth forty-four. It was from this same historic port in Southampton that the Pilgrims had boarded the *Mayflower* and headed to the New World.

While in port, supplies were brought aboard and the *Titanic* was prepared for her first voyage to the New World. The ship's pantry had 75,000 pounds of fresh meat, 40,000 eggs, 2,200 pounds of coffee, 200 barrels of flour, 2.5 tons of tomatoes, 16,000 lemons, 15,000 bottles of mineral water and 50 boxes of grapefruit. For dining purposes, there were 12,000 ice cream plates, 8,000 dinner forks, 12,000 dinner plates and 8,000 cut-glass tumblers. In addition, there were 6,000 tablecloths, 4,000 aprons and 40,000 miscellaneous items. The *Titanic* also carried general cargo, including 12 cases of ostrich plumes, 300 cases of shelled walnuts, 63 cases of champagne and one new Renault. The fastest way to transport general cargo across the ocean was on regularly scheduled ocean liners. The *Titanic* and other ships also carried the royal mail, thus the prefix RMS (Royal Mail Ship) before the name *Titanic*.

Many of the crew members lived in Southampton, England, and were hired just prior to sailing. There were 899 crew members, and as in the English class system, they ranged in rank from the captain down to the stokers who fed the furnaces. There were also musicians, postal clerks, cooks, wireless operators, seamen, firemen, engineers, stewards, bedroom stewards, chefs, a masseuse and a matron who was a chaperone for the single women. The crew members ran the ship and served the needs of the passengers.

April 10 was sailing day. At 7:30 a.m., Captain Smith boarded the *Titanic*. At 8:00 a.m., the blue ensign was hoisted at the stern. The blue ensign was flown because Captain Smith was a Royal Navy Reserve officer. This flag differed from the red ensign flag sometimes termed the "red duster," which was flown on most British ocean liners. The White Star pennant went up on the main mast. Special boat trains were making runs bringing passengers from London's Waterloo Station to the White Star docks. At 9:30 a.m., the second-class and third-class passengers walked up the gangplank to board the ship. Each class had its own separate entrance to board the ship. The first-class passengers arrived at 11:30 a.m. Whereas first-class and second-class passengers were treated as honored guests entering a grand hotel, third-class passengers were given a quick medical examination to make sure they did not have any health problems. Indeed, the welcome received by the passengers was determined by the class for which they had bought tickets.

Of course, first-class staterooms were beautiful, second-class less so and third-class rooms were quite spartan but certainly better than third-class accommodations on other ships, which still used the term "steerage." More than half of these third-class passengers did not speak English; therefore, it must have been a challenge for them to find their way around the massive ship. Although their cabins were modest, and there were only two bathtubs for seven hundred people, many of the occupants were excited at the prospect of a new life in America. They soon expected to be welcomed by the Statue of Liberty as the *Titanic* entered New York Harbor for the first time. In fact, someone even suggested that the ship was so large that she might pull the Statue of Liberty off its pedestal when she sailed by it.

When the passengers boarded the new ship, they must have been overwhelmed by its beauty and facilities, including elevators, the Café

Parisian, a magnificent grand staircase that was sixty feet high, a hospital, reading and writing rooms, Turkish baths, a promenade deck, a squash court, a gymnasium, a darkroom to develop photographs, a barbershop, a swimming pool, a smoking room for men and a kennel for the nine dogs and a cage for the one canary making the trip. Indeed, the sheer size and luxury of the *Titanic* made people gasp. It was an overwhelming sight. Three thousand miles away, the *Times Dispatch* carried this story on its front page: "The new White Star liner *Titanic*, the biggest vessel afloat, started from Southampton on her maiden voyage to New York."

Around noon, Captain Smith gave the order, and the *Titanic*'s triple-tone whistle sounded. The sound could be heard throughout the harbor as hundreds of well-wishers watched the ship leave. The beautiful ship that had become a tourist attraction while at Southampton was on her way. Then, disaster almost struck! The power of the *Titanic*'s propellers snapped the mooring ropes of the steamer SS *New York*, and the *New York* swung out toward the *Titanic*. Immediately, Captain Smith ordered full astern, and the sudden burst of water from the *Titanic*'s port propeller helped push the *New York* away before it crashed into the *Titanic*. But for the quick thinking and actions of Captain Smith, the two ships would have collided. They missed a collision by about four feet.

Many passengers saw the near miss as a bad omen. In fact, the *Olympic*, under Captain Smith's command, had been involved in a serious collision with the British ship HMS *Hawke*. It was frequently suggested that Captain Smith and other captains had not learned how to maneuver these massive new ships, which were larger than any previous ships under their command. The *Titanic* continued her passage down Southampton waters. As mealtime approached, the bugler sounded "The Roast Beef of Old England," which was the traditional meal call for the Royal Navy, as well as English ocean liners. The song contained these lines:

When good Queen Elizabeth sat on the throne,
Ere coffee, or tea, or such slip-slops were known.
The world was in terror if e'er she did frown.
O! the Roast Beef of Old England!
And O! for old England's Roast Beef!

Following the departure from Southampton and the near miss with the *New York*, the *Titanic* arrived in Cherbourg, France. The waiting passengers had arrived on a special "Train Transalantique" from Paris. Because of her size, the *Titanic* could not dock at Cherbourg, so smaller vessels brought passengers to the ship. One passenger commented on the wealthy women on board by writing, "Looking over the passenger list, I only find three or four people I know but there are a number of ostentatious American women, the scourge of any place they infest, and worse on shipboard then anywhere. Many of them carry tiny dogs and lead their husbands around like pet lambs." The *Titanic* left Cherbourg at 8:10 p.m. after about a two-hour stay and headed to Queenstown, Ireland, which was the traditional final stop for ships headed to North America.

On April 11, the *Titanic* arrived in Queenstown Harbor. Horrified, some of the passengers saw a soot-covered face peering out of the fourth funnel, which was a dummy funnel. Since most of the passengers would not have known the funnel was a dummy, they were horrified by the sight of a man coming out of a funnel and felt it was an evil omen. At least one lady thought it was the "Angel of Death." What the passengers did not see was a smoldering fire in one of the coal bunkers. An even greater concern should have been that the *Titanic* did not have any lifeboat drills. It was said that Captain Smith reportedly never had lifeboat drills on any of the ships under his command.

Because of its size, the *Titanic* could not dock at Queenstown, so passengers were again ferried out to the ship as they had been in Cherbourg. Once the passengers were on board, the *Titanic* gave three long, mournful blasts on her whistle, followed by a short blast. The *Titanic* put to sea with approximately 2,200 passengers and crew members on board, including such wealthy and famous people as John Jacob Astor and Madeleine Astor, Molly Brown, Isidor and Ida Straus, George Widener, Benjamin Guggenheim, Charles Hays, John Thayer, the Countess of Rothes, Sir Cosmo Duff Gordon, Lady Duff Gordon, Major Archibald Butt, Colonel Archibald Gracie IV and the movie star Dorothy Gibson. The *Titanic* was like a floating palace filled with royalty; it was the gathering place of the rich and famous of the western world. She was the very essence of the song with the lyrics, "Rule Britannia, Britannia rules the waves. Britons never, never, never shall be slaves."

The passengers on the *Titanic* came from over thirty countries. Within days, more than three-quarters of those on board the ship would be dead. But death at sea was not likely on their minds when they left Europe in the most beautiful ship created by the mind of man. As the *Titanic* steamed out to sea, an iceberg floated south as the *Titanic* headed west. The great ship gathered speed, and Eugene Daly stood on the promenade deck and

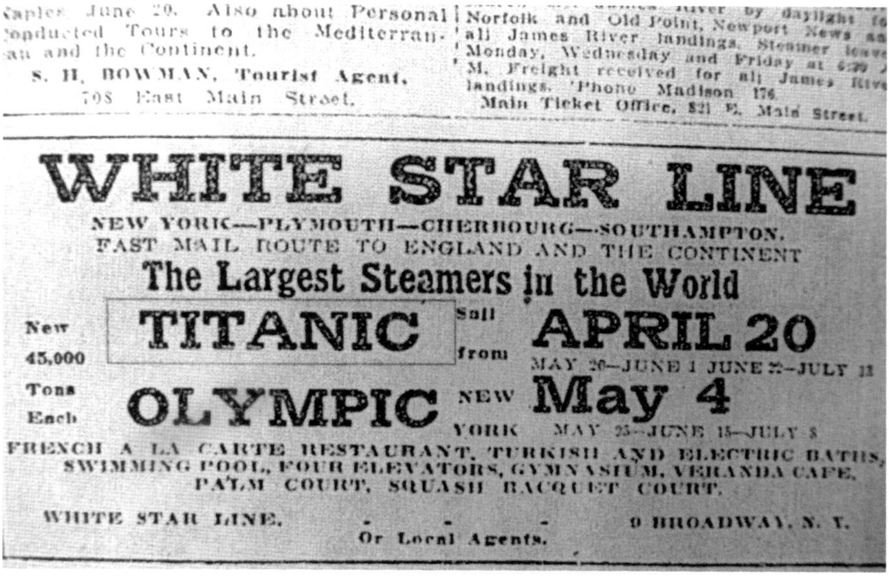

Advertisement in the *Times Dispatch* announcing the April 20, 1912 sailing of the *Titanic*. *Courtesy of the National Archives.*

played "Erin's Lament" on his Irish bagpipes. Slowly, Ireland faded into the distance. On the foremast of the *Titanic* were the "stars and stripes" that were to signal her destination to all who saw her at sea.

As the *Titanic* put out to sea, there was an advertisement in the Richmond newspaper for tickets for the *Titanic* sailing on April 20, 1912, from New York. The advertisement pointed out that the ship had a French a la carte restaurant and Turkish and electric baths, along with other comforts for the traveling public. It was stated over and over that this ship was the largest steamer in the world. By April 20, the *Titanic* had sunk and bodies were being pulled out of the ocean. There would be no sailing on April 20; there would be only a weeping world.

Chapter 5
Out to Sea

They that go down to the sea in ships, that do business in great waters.
—Psalm 107:23

In 1912, the North Atlantic was the most dangerous ocean in the world. Its sea lanes were filled with ships that could collide if someone made a slight misjudgment. There were also the constant challenges provided by nature, including icebergs, rough seas, tropical hurricanes and thick fog. Across the years, thousands of ships had sailed into the North Atlantic never to be seen or heard from again. Samuel Johnson observed, "An ocean voyage was much like being thrown in jail with the added opportunity of being drowned."

The dangers of an Atlantic crossing were well known, but less well known were some of the strange—if not eerie—events that had taken place prior to the *Titanic* being built. For example, books were written and comments made that seemed to predict a tragic outcome to the *Titanic*'s voyage to the New World. William Thomas Stead, in 1886, wrote about two ocean liners that collided in the North Atlantic. One of the ships sank, and many lives were lost because of a lack of lifeboats. Stead then commented, "This is exactly what might take place, and will take place, if liners are sent to sea short of boats." A few years later, he wrote a story about a ship hitting an iceberg. Ironically, William Thomas Stead was a passenger on the *Titanic*. He did not survive. He seemed to have written the story of his own death.

A similar theme can be found in an 1898 novel written by Morgan Robertson entitled *Futility*. The novel is about an ocean liner named the *Titan*. The *Titan*

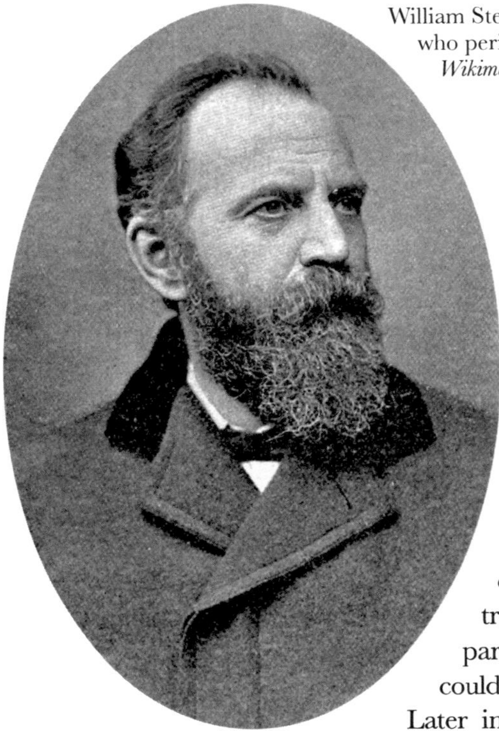

William Stead, newspaper editor and spiritualist, who perished on the *Titanic*. *Courtesy of Wikimedia Commons.*

had many similarities with the *Titanic*, and like the *Titanic*, she struck an iceberg and foundered, losing half the people aboard because of an insufficient number of lifeboats. In the first paragraph, Robertson wrote, "She was the largest craft afloat and the greatest of the works of man. In her construction and maintenance were involved every science, profession, and trade known to civilization." This paragraph about the fictional *Titan* could also have applied to the *Titanic*. Later in the book, the author describes the *Titan*'s collision with an iceberg. He wrote: "Seventy-five thousand tons—dead weight—rushing through the fog at the rate of fifty feet a second had hurled itself at an iceberg. The ship [*Titan*] rose out of the water higher and higher…she heeled, overbalanced, and crashed down on her side, the starboard side." Many people agreed that Morgan Robertson's book was the closest thing to a prophetic writing about the *Titanic*.

Celia Thaxter wrote a poem in 1887 entitled "A Tryst." It told a similar story in these lines:

From out of the desolation of the North
An iceberg took its way.
From its detaining comrades breaking forth,
And traveling night and day.

Was not the weltering waste of water wide?
Enough for both to sail?
What drew the two together o'er the tide?
Fair ship and iceberg pale?

Scarcely her crew had time to clutch despair
So swift the work was done:
Ere their pale lips could form a speechless prayer,
They perished everyone!

Emil Taussig was a passenger on the *Titanic*. He had a lifelong interest in ocean travel and was concerned that ships did not carry enough lifeboats for all of their passengers. He wrote numerous letters to the United States Steam Ship Inspection Service expressing his concerns. His concerns were not addressed. He went down on the *Titanic*.

In 1912, *The White Ghost of Disaster* was written by Thornton Jenkins Hains under the pen name Mayn Clew Garnett. The story told of a ship that hit an iceberg and of the many lives that were lost. The story appeared in *Popular Magazine* and was being put on the newsstand the day the *Titanic* struck the iceberg.

There were other events that seem, in retrospect, to be unusual. For various reasons, a number of people did not make the trip on the *Titanic*. One of the best known was J.P. Morgan, who had to cancel because of a last-minute business commitment. Father Frank Browne had made the first two stops on the *Titanic*. He had an opportunity to sail on the ship to America when his Jesuit superiors ordered him to "get off that ship." He obeyed and lived. A crew member was ready to sail when "some sort of feeling" came over him. He got off the ship. Henry Wilde, the chief officer of the *Titanic*, wrote his sister a letter that was mailed from Queenstown, Ireland, on April 11, 1912. He commented, "I don't like this ship…I have a queer feeling about it." He died after assisting women and children into lifeboats.

Some of the other passengers also had good reasons to cancel their reservations. A steel mill operator, Henry Clay Frick, canceled his reservations when his wife sprained her ankle. And George Vanderbilt, an American millionaire, canceled the reservation for himself and his wife because his mother had an aversion to maiden voyages. He made the decision even though their luggage was already on the *Titanic*. Their servant, however, stayed with the luggage and was not saved. The United States ambassador to France might well have died on the *Titanic*, but he could not leave France because his replacement had not arrived. Apparently, a number of people had unexplained, uneasy feelings about the *Titanic* or were saved from disaster by a fortunate quirk of fate. At least fifty-five passengers who had tickets did not board the ship, and twenty-two crew members did not sail on her for various reasons. It was reported that one crew member "jumped ship" at the last minute.

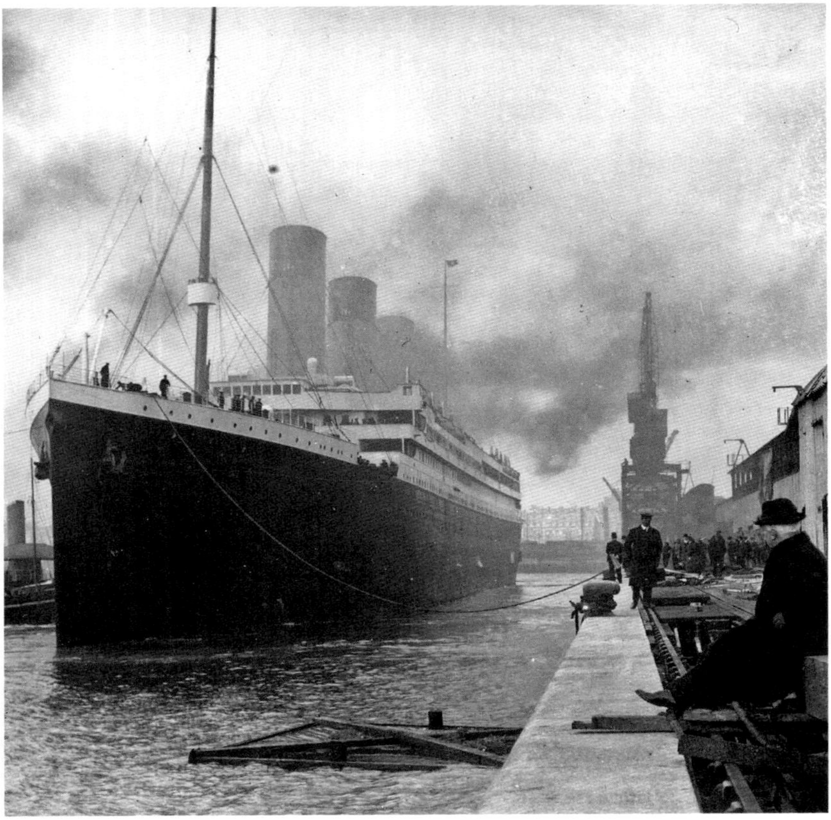

Titanic prior to sailing. *Courtesy of Wikimedia Commons.*

It was also reported that even the rats seemed to be uneasy and unsettled. Ironically, the ship's cat, Jenny, jumped off before the *Titanic* sailed and took her kittens with her. It was considered a bad omen for the ship's cat to leave a ship before sailing. Sailors could be superstitious, and there was enough going on to make them quite uneasy. By tradition, sailors would "knock on wood" before getting on a ship. Of course, the saying comes from the days of wooden ships, but seamen still did it for good luck. The *Titanic* would need a lot of good luck.

Most of the passengers were unaware of these strange occurrences as they enjoyed sailing across the Atlantic. Of course, if the *Titanic* had arrived in New York safely, these eerie events might have never been recalled, but in retrospect, they seemed to be precursors of disaster. It should also be noted that the one canary on the ship flew off in France.

Chapter 6

Full Speed Ahead

O God, our help in ages past,
Our hope for years to come,
Our shelter from the stormy blast,
And our eternal home.
—Issac Watts

Lead, Kindly Light, amidst th'encircling gloom,
Lead Thou me on!
—John Henry Newman

Leaving the sight of land for the last time, the *Titanic* steamed toward New York. Lawrence Beesley, a passenger, commented that there was little of interest for the first two days except for the calm sea and the somewhat "fresh" weather. Beesley wrote, "Each morning, the sun rose behind us in a sky of circular clouds stretching round the horizon in long, narrow streaks and rose tier upon tier above the sky line, red and pink, and fading from pink to white as the sun rose higher in the sky."

The *Titanic* was making good—but not record—time on her maiden voyage. There were numerous comments from the passengers that the *Titanic* was the most comfortable ship they had been on and that they preferred the slower speed to the faster speed of some of the Cunard liners. One passenger commented that "the slower speed lessened vibration, because the faster boats would bore through the waves with a twisted, screw-like motion instead of the straight

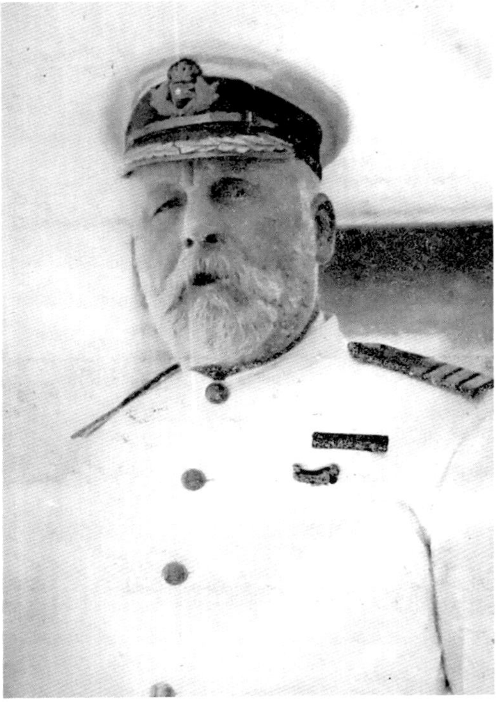

Captain Edward J. Smith, who commanded the *Titanic*. *Courtesy of Wikimedia Commons.*

up-and-down swing of the *Titanic*." Based on the first days at sea, White Star's decision to put comfort over speed seemed to have been vindicated. But the passengers might not have enjoyed their voyage so much if they had known that Captain Smith had been receiving repeated warnings of ice in the area that the *Titanic* was to sail through and that he was paying little—if any—attention to them. He did not slow down. Ironically, in the *Titanic*'s Chart Room was posted this note: "Overconfidence should be specially guarded against."

April 14 was a Sunday, and divine services were held in the Saloon, led by Captain Smith, who read some prayers. Hymns were selected from the interdenominational *White Star Line Hymn and Prayer Book*. The service ended with the hymn "O, God, Our Help in Ages Past." About this same time, Father Thomas Byles conducted a Mass for the Catholic passengers on board.

Following the services, the passengers who wandered out on deck noticed that the weather was much colder. Otherwise, the day was uneventful. During the evening, there was a hymn-sing at 8:30 p.m., led by the Reverend Ernest C. Carter, an Episcopal priest. During the service, people would mention a hymn, Reverend Carter would tell about how the hymn came to be written and then the people would sing it. The service was called a "hymn-sing-song." Over one hundred passengers participated in the service.

Two of the hymns focused on travel at sea. One of the hymns sung was "Lead, Kindly Light." This hymn was written by John Henry Newman while he was in deep despair on a ship bound for Marseilles. There was no wind, and the ship was not moving. To deal with his impatience and his search for a purpose in his life, he wrote these lines:

Lead, Kindly Light, amidst th'encircling gloom,
Lead Thou me on!
The night is dark, and I am far from home.
Lead Thou me on.

In the case of the *Titanic*, it was a very dark night, and the souls on board were indeed far from home.

The final hymn for the evening was "Eternal Father, Strong to Save." This hymn was written in 1860 by William Whiting, who was inspired by the perils of the sea as related in Psalm 107. The writer was the headmaster of an English school, and he wrote it for a student who had confided in him his fear of the sea. Reverend Carter introduced the hymn by saying, "In this ship we are not in peril, but others may be. Let us sing this hymn for them." The hymn contains this verse:

Eternal Father, Strong to save.
Whose arm hath bound the restless wave,
Who bid'st the mighty Ocean deep
Its own appointed limits keep;
Oh, hear us when we cry to Thee,
For those in peril on the sea.

Many passengers would also recall the "Prayers for Those at Sea." Reverend Carter repeated these lines from the *Book of Common Prayer* following the singing of hymns: "O, Eternal Lord God, who alone speediest out the heavens and rulest the raging of the seas; who hast compassed the waters with bounds until day and night come to an end; Be pleased to receive into thy Almighty and most gracious protection the persons of us thy servants."

Those who had sung and folded their hands in prayer did not know it, but in less than four hours, they would be in the "perils of the sea." Indeed, one passenger at the service commented that the hymns selected focused on disasters at sea.

While the passengers were singing, the ship was receiving numerous reports of icebergs in the area through which she was to sail. Beginning at 9:00 a.m. on April 14, there were iceberg reports from the RMS *Caronia*, SS *Baltic*, *Amerika* and SS *Californian*, but the *Titanic* continued at twenty-two and a half knots. With warnings ignored, the *Titanic* headed for an ice belt seventy-eight miles across her track.

While the *Titanic* was steaming west, Archibald Gracie returned a book to the ship's library. The book was by Mary Johnston and was entitled *Old*

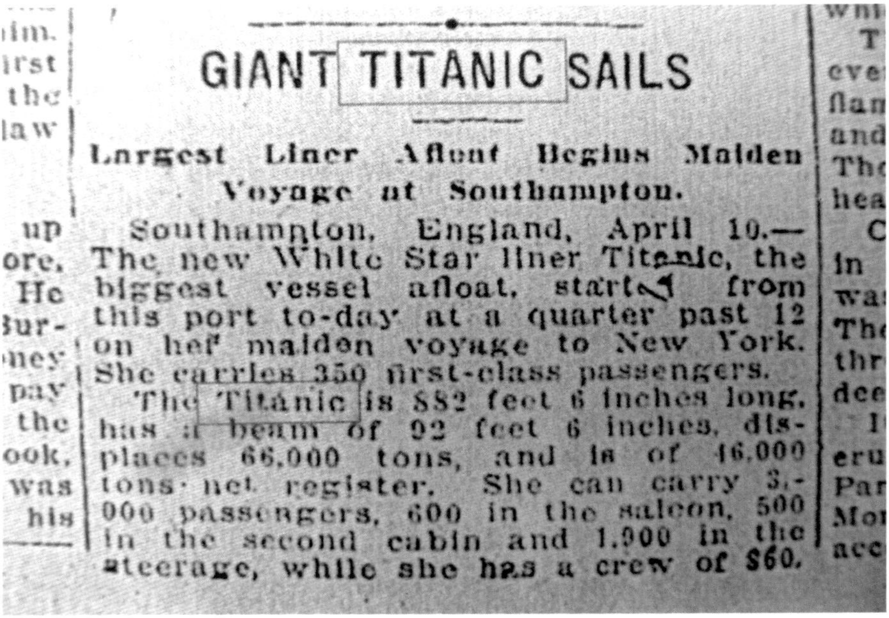

GIANT TITANIC SAILS

Largest Liner Afloat Begins Maiden Voyage at Southampton.

Southampton, England, April 10.—The new White Star liner Titanic, the biggest vessel afloat, started from this port to-day at a quarter past 12 on her maiden voyage to New York. She carries 350 first-class passengers.

The Titanic is 882 feet 6 inches long, has a beam of 92 feet 6 inches, displaces 66,000 tons, and is of 46,000 tons net register. She can carry 3,000 passengers, 600 in the saloon, 500 in the second cabin and 1,900 in the steerage, while she has a crew of 860.

A story in the *Times Dispatch* announcing the sailing of the *Titanic*. *Author's collection.*

Dominion. For a time, Mary Johnston had lived in Richmond, and the book focused on the early history of Virginia. Several weeks later, Archibald Gracie commented that the stories of escaping slaves in the book could not compare in any way to his escape from the *Titanic.*

While the *Titanic* was sailing across the Atlantic, Richmonders were reading about the steamer *Ontario*, which had been beached to save her passengers. Those rescued were taken to New London, Connecticut. The same newspaper carried the story of an excursion steamer that sank in the Nile River. It was reported that many lives were lost. Seeing two stories of shipwrecks on the front page of the same morning newspaper was a precursor to what would be on the front pages in a few days and would remain front-page news for several weeks.

On April 11, there was a front-page story in the *Times Dispatch* with the headline "Giant *Titanic* Sails." The same issue reported that Clara Barton, the founder of the American Red Cross, had died. She was known as the "Angel of Mercy." In the days ahead, there would be many angels of mercy providing comfort "for those in peril on the sea."

Chapter 7
"God Himself Cannot Sink This Ship"

'Twas on a fatal Sunday night.
When all was calm and your lights were shining bright,
All of a sudden there was a crash, a cry, 'tis all too late
For thou, oh, great Titanic, *has met thy fate.*
—*Chrystal Mohr*

While Richmonders reviewed the day's events in their Sunday newspapers, the passengers on the *Titanic* slept, as the ship continued slicing through the North Atlantic at its highest speed of the voyage. Although unconfirmed, there were those who believed that she was trying to break the *Olympic*'s record in reaching New York and that J. Bruce Ismay, the president of the White Star Line, was encouraging such an effort. Based on the many ice warnings he had received, Captain Smith knew that the *Titanic* was approaching an ice field, but he did not order the ship to slow down, nor did he increase the number of lookouts at the most dangerous part of the voyage. Captain Smith went to his cabin after an evening meal with some of the passengers but requested that he be summoned to the bridge if the situation changed.

Although it seems illogical to speed toward an ice field knowing of the danger, it was the general policy of North Atlantic captains not to slow down when approaching ice. Instead, they would depend on the lookouts and wireless communications from other ships to let them know of any danger ahead. And when danger was spotted, it was believed that those in command could avoid a collision by promptly changing course. This was risky behavior, but it was the standard operating procedure in 1912.

In command when Captain Smith retired for the night was Second Officer Charles H. Lightoller, who took the precaution to advise the two lookouts to keep "a sharp eye for ice." Unfortunately, these two men did not have binoculars to aid them in spotting danger. The binoculars were locked in a cabinet, and the officer with the key was no longer on board the ship. The lookouts stared at a calm sea on a moonless night. Lightoller would later comment that in his fifteen years at sea, he had never before witnessed these conditions. With no waves to break on the ice and with no moonlight to improve visibility, the two lookouts had nothing to aid them but their own vision—and perhaps luck. The safety of everyone on board was dependent on the two lookouts braving the cold winds in the frigid crow's nest, which was fifty feet above the deck. They were truly the eyes of the ship.

In the radio room, a message was received at 10:45 p.m. from the captain of the nearby *Californian*. The ship had stopped because of the ice, and the wireless operator on duty sent an ice warning to other ships. Jack Phillips, the wireless operator on duty on the *Titanic*, was sending passengers' personal messages. When he got the ice warning, he wired "Shut Up" to the other wireless operator. Being tired and with a backlog of personal messages to send, he did not want to be interrupted by the loud wireless communications from a nearby ship that deafened him. Therefore, he continued to send personal messages for passengers instead of listening and taking messages to the bridge that could have saved the *Titanic* from a fatal encounter with an iceberg in about forty-five minutes. At 11:00 p.m., Charles Lightoller was relieved on the bridge by First Officer William Murdoch. The two officers stood together until Murdoch's eyes had become adjusted to the dark, cold night. Five hours later, only one of these men would be alive.

Around 11:30 p.m., the two lookouts in the crow's nest saw a misty haze in the distance, but nothing else. A quartermaster reported seeing "what we call whiskers around the light…that is very minute splinters of ice like myriads of colored lights." The unaided vision of the lookouts could not penetrate the haze to see if there was anything lurking behind it. Then it happened.

At 11:40 p.m., lookout Frederick Fleet "saw a black iceberg that he described as 'about the size of two tables'" looming five hundred yards in front of the *Titanic*. The ancient ice mountain was dead ahead of the fast-moving ship. Frederick Fleet rang the brass bell in the crow's nest three times to warn of the iceberg, and then he telephoned the bridge and reported, "Iceberg right ahead!" Responding to the emergency, First Officer Murdoch ordered the quartermaster to turn the ship's wheel hard a starboard, which would swing the ship to port, and then he telegraphed the engine room, "Stop, full speed astern" and closed the watertight doors. He had done everything that a mortal could do to prevent a collision and save the ship. But his efforts were doomed to failure.

The two lookouts saw the *Titanic* swing slowly, very slowly, to port to go around the iceberg, but it was too late. Forty seconds after receiving the message from the crow's nest, there was the fatal meeting of steel and ice. The great ship did not hit the iceberg head on, but rather about three hundred feet of the ship below the waterline scraped against a part of the iceberg that was under water and penetrated the first five watertight compartments on the starboard side. The contact between the *Titanic* and the iceberg lasted about ten seconds.

In retrospect, Murdoch should have struck the iceberg head on. It would have crushed the bow, but the ship would not have sunk. This is the course of action recommended by the *1910 Edition of Knight's Modern Seamanship*. The book stated: "To turn away and slow is the surest possible way of bringing about a collision." Yet, it is difficult and illogical to plow into an iceberg when there was the hope you could miss it. But that was the procedure that should have been followed, and by not following it, the *Titanic* was doomed.

Within minutes, Captain Smith, who had felt the collision, was on the bridge and was told the ship had struck an iceberg and what steps had been taken. He then ordered the ship stopped. With the powerful engines stopped, steam was released that made a screaming noise that certainly unsettled the passengers and made it difficult to be heard on deck. The escaping steam was the first agonizing cry from a dying ship. He then ordered an inspection of the ship. Although large chunks of ice rained down on the *Titanic*'s forward well deck, many passengers and crew members were unaware of the collision.

Passengers' awareness of what had happened depended on a number of variables, including where they were when the collision occurred and whether they were asleep or awake. Some comments on the collision with the iceberg were as follows: "It was as if we went over about a thousand marbles"; "There was a slowing down"; "There was the sound of rending metal"; "It was like a dog shaking a kitten"; "It was like someone tearing a long strip of calico"; "It was a rumbling, scraping noise"; "a slight shock"; "a tremendous noise"; "a faint grinding jar"; "a slight sway"; and the sound of silence from not hearing the engines. Some passengers and crew members who had experience on ships thought the ship must have lost a propeller.

The postal clerks did not have to hear anything to know of the disaster, as icy water was already pouring in on them and the mail bags were starting to float. These clerks, one of whom was from North Carolina, were desperately trying to save the mail. Water also poured into the boiler room on the starboard side like a "roar of thunder." Within minutes, there was ten feet of water in boiler room 6. These men were among the first to know that the *Titanic* was doomed.

After an inspection of the stricken ship and a conversation with Thomas Andrews, Captain Smith knew the *Titanic* was doomed. So much damage had been done by scraping the iceberg that the watertight compartments would soon flood and take the ship down. Andrews gave the *Titanic* two hours to live. After a brief delay, Captain Smith ordered the lifeboats uncovered and made ready to receive passengers. However, there were not enough lifeboats to save all of the people, and the captain and Andrews knew it. The decision to be more concerned with passenger comfort than passenger safety would now cost over one thousand lives.

With his ship slowly sinking, Captain Smith apparently had no plan as to how to save as many passengers as possible, and there had been no lifeboat drills. It has been suggested that the reason he never gave a general order to evacuate the ship was because he knew there were not enough lifeboats and a general evacuation order would reveal this fact and perhaps cause a panic. For a while, most people on the *Titanic* did not know its death warrant had been signed. Indeed, the news of the damage to the ship was kept from the passengers. When the passengers sought to find out what had happened, they were assured that there was no reason to be concerned. But when the passengers saw unusual activity among the officers and crew, they surmised that something was not right.

The death of many of the passengers and crew members was virtually inevitable for a number of reasons. The *Titanic* had only enough lifeboats for about half the passengers on board; there had not been a lifeboat drill; there was an inadequate number of crew members to man the boats; there was an unfounded concern that if the lifeboats were fully loaded, they would break apart; and the crew and passengers had not been given a specific lifeboat assignment. It could be suggested that the notion of the ship being unsinkable had caused the captain to ignore basic safety precaution.

As the crisis deepened on Sunday, April 15, at 12:10 a.m., Captain Smith told wireless operator Jack Phillips to send out a call for assistance. The first wireless call from the *Titanic* was as follows: "CQD MGY 41.46 N. 50.14 W." CQD was the international call for assistance, MGY was the *Titanic*'s call letters and the ship's position was 41.46 N 50.14 W. Later, Jack Phillips would use the new distress call SOS, instead of CQD, after the comment was made that this might be his last chance to use it. The *Titanic* was one of the first ships to use the new emergency call. Fortunately for those on the *Titanic*, the wireless set on the ship was one of the best available and Jack Phillips was an experienced operator.

While the *Titanic* was sending out distress calls, the RMS *Carpathia* was sailing to the Mediterranean from New York City. She had pulled away from Cunard's Pier 54 on April 11, 1912. The vast majority of her passengers were traveling in third class. In command of the *Carpathia* was Captain Arthur Rostron. Because of his ability to make quick decisions, other Cunard officers and crew referred to him as the "electric spark." Unlike many seamen, he did not curse or smoke, and he was well known as a deeply religious man who frequently prayed for guidance in difficult situations. For what was soon to happen, Arthur Rostron was certainly the best person to be in command of a rescue operation.

On board the *Carpathia*, Harold Cottam, the wireless operator, was trying to get a knot out of his shoelace before turning off the ship's wireless for the night. While trying to get the knot out, the silence of his cabin was broken by a wireless distress call from the *Titanic*. At 12:25 a.m., Cottam responded to the distress call, and Phillips replied, "Come at once. We have struck a berg and require immediate assistance. It's a CQD old man. Position 41.46 N 50.14 W." The *Carpathia*'s wireless operator wanted to know if the captain should be notified. Phillips responded in the affirmative. Once notified, the *Carpathia* quickly altered course. She was fifty-eight miles away, but she was coming as rapidly as possible. Soon, the *Titanic* started to lower its lifeboats but only after some prodding of Captain Smith by Second Officer Lightoller. There were those who felt that Captain Smith was in some sort of trance and could not deal with a situation of this magnitude.

Many people refused to get in the lifeboats since even the damaged *Titanic* seemed to be much safer than an open, wooden lifeboat. And there were those who probably still thought the *Titanic* was unsinkable. Indeed, one crew member quipped, "God himself could not sink this ship." As the lifeboats began to be loaded, the rule was "women and children first," which had become a tradition at sea as far as Great Britain was concerned. Its origins are still compelling.

In 1885, the British steamer HMS *Birkenhead* was wrecked off the coast of Southern Africa after hitting rocks. Richmonders read in the *Daily Dispatch* that "her majesty's steamer, the *Birkenhead*, was filled with many soldiers when it was torn apart two or three miles from the shores of Southern Africa." Of the 636 people aboard, only 184 survived. The story that Richmonders read related that the soldiers on board stood at attention while the women and children got into lifeboats. There were no lifeboats for most of these men. Most of them died in a futile effort to reach the shore. Of the valor of the soldiers, Rudyard Kipling wrote:

To stand and be still
To the Birken'ead Drill
Is a damn tough bullet to chew.

This practice gave rise to the "women and children first" protocol, and this rule became known as the "Birkenhead Drill." Over fifty years later, the "Birkenhead Drill" would have a major impact on those who stood on the sloping decks of the sinking *Titanic*.

Even though it was a noble tradition, the "Birkenhead Drill" was not always followed on the *Titanic*. A man on the starboard side, where the odd-numbered lifeboats were located, had a better chance of survival because First Officer Murdoch did not strictly enforce the women-and-children rule, whereas Second Officer Lightoller on the port side generally enforced it. While this was taking place, the Reverend John Harper, a Baptist preacher, "pleaded that along with the women and children, those people who had not been saved [from hell] also be accorded a place in a lifeboat so they would have a chance to be saved by the Lord and Savior Jesus Christ." The fact that there had been no lifeboat drills made the loading of the lifeboats a real challenge. Many lifeboats were lowered with many vacant seats. As the lifeboats were being loaded, the *Titanic* was firing rockets into the air to attract the attention of any nearby ships. The nearby *Californian*, which was about ten miles away, saw the rockets but did not respond to aid the *Titanic*. If the *Californian* had responded, many people could have been saved. Her failure to respond continues to be a mystery to this day.

As the *Titanic*'s fate became more obvious, some men jumped into the lifeboats while a few covered their heads with shawls to appear to be women. One man who was saved was J. Bruce Ismay, chairman of the White Star Line. He got into a lifeboat and survived while women and children drowned. He had saved his life but lost the respect of most of the world. He would bear tremendous criticism for the rest of his life.

As the situation got more desperate, people started to rush the boats to get one of the few precious seats. Boats were no longer being lowered with empty seats. Men whose fortunes could buy railroads could not buy a seat in a wooden lifeboat. While many women were saved, some women refused to leave their husbands and chose to follow their husbands even into death in the freezing water. Mrs. Isidor Straus reportedly said to her husband, "We have been together for many years. Where you go, I go." They died as they had lived: together. Lifeboat 8 was lowered without them.

Tragically, over a dozen couples were spending their honeymoons on the *Titanic*. One groom, a devout Christian Scientist, would not join his wife in the lifeboat. He quoted Mary Baker Eddy, the founder of Christian Science, by saying, "Divine love has always met and always will meet every human need." Some husbands told their wives that they would get in another lifeboat when they probably knew there were no other lifeboats. Is it wrong to tell a lie to save a life? Some women, who did not believe

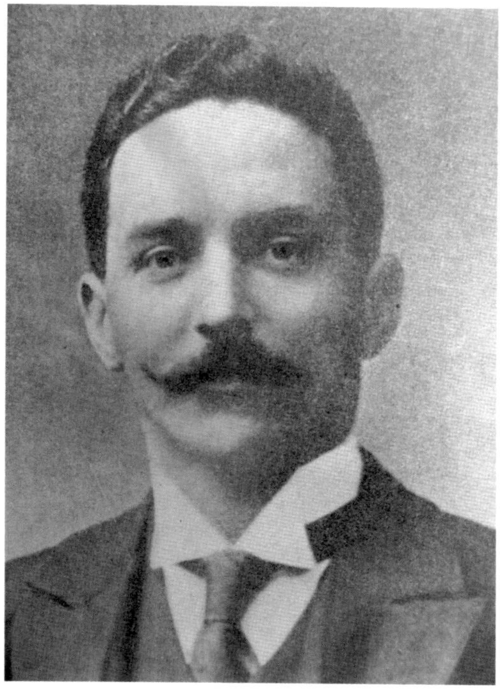

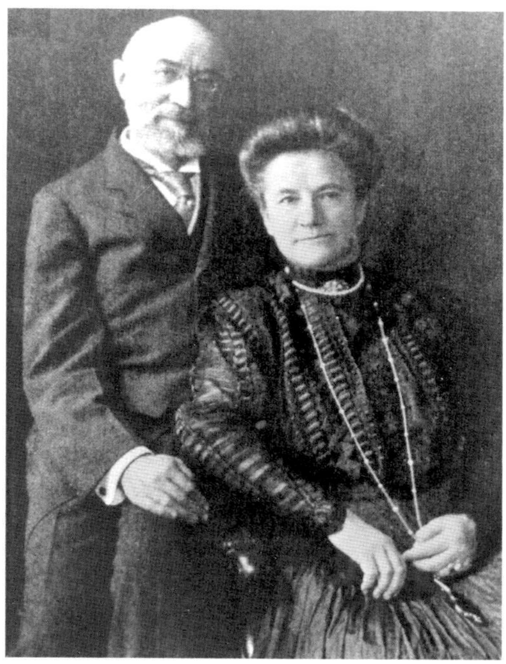

Top: J. Bruce Ismay, chairman of the board of the White Star Line. *Courtesy of the National Archives.*

Right: Ida and Isidor Straus, who died together on the *Titanic*. *Courtesy of Wikimedia Commons.*

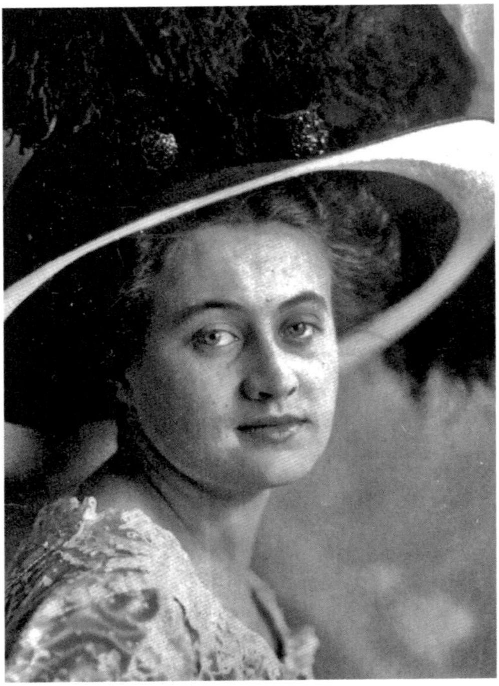

Dorothy Gibson, a *Titanic* survivor who starred in the movie *Saved from the* Titanic. *Courtesy of Wikimedia Commons.*

they could be saved, tossed their children into the lifeboats. One woman who was saved was Dorothy Gibson, an American actress. Once she reached shore, she made a movie about the *Titanic* wearing the same clothes she wore when she was rescued. The film, *Saved from the* Titanic, was released near the end of April and was a tremendous success.

Even as it became obvious that the *Titanic* was sinking, many people still refused to leave. At 2:05 p.m., the last lifeboat was lowered into the cold Atlantic and with it virtually all hope of survival for those who remained on board the *Titanic*. Thomas Andrews now awaited death with his life jacket tossed on a table. Perhaps he thought about the debate over the number of lifeboats. Those who had attended the evening "hymn-sing-song" surely knew that they were now in "peril on the sea."

As the *Carpathia* continued to speed toward the position of the *Titanic*, her wireless operator received the last wireless message from the *Titanic*. It was: "Come as quickly as possible, old man, our engine room is filling up to the boilers." The failure to hear any additional calls from the *Titanic* told a very sad story to the crew of the *Carpathia*.

Chapter 8
Until Death Us Do Part

As the mighty ship was sinking
In the cold and icy sea,
The last that the band was heard to play
Was "Nearer, My God, to Thee."
—Unknown

Those left on the *Titanic* facing almost certain death confronted it in many different ways. Some people got drunk, some read books, some locked themselves in their staterooms, some just stood on the deck and smoked a final cigar and some played cards. Some men dressed in their finest evening attire so they could "go down like gentlemen," and married couples held hands "until death us do part." Many passengers and crew members watched the waters of death creep slowly up the decks until it swept them into eternity. Others turned to Almighty God for comfort as they "walked through the valley of the shadow of death." Kate Buss summed up the feeling of many passengers when she said, "I was alone with God, and whatever happened must be for the best. I felt as I have felt before when death has stared me in the face, that I had to do nothing but wait on God's will."

As the waters closed over the ship, many people heard the *Titanic*'s band playing "Alexander's Rag Time Band" and other popular songs. As the water continued to pull the *Titanic* down to her grave, the musicians stopped playing popular songs and started to play Sarah Adams's hymn of faith, "Nearer, My God, to Thee." Ada Clark recalled, "All the musicians were kneeling while they played and there floated out across the water the strains of 'Nearer, My God, to Thee.'"

Wallace Hartley, who was leading the musicians in an effort to keep the passengers calm, always said that if he faced death aboard a ship, he would play "Nearer, My God, to Thee." Regardless of what subsequent historians have claimed, Richmonders believed the last notes that floated from the dying ship were "Nearer, My God, to Thee." W. T. Stead, who had predicted the collision of a ship and an iceberg, had listed "Nearer, My God, to Thee" as one of his favorite hymns. In one of his many books, he wrote, "This hymn is as dear to the peasant as it is to the prince." He termed it "the most popular hymn among all sorts and conditions of men." Perhaps he heard it as the cold Atlantic carried him into eternity and "Nearer, My God, to Thee."

In the book my great-grandmother read by Jay Mowbray, the following lines are included: "Survivors who were nearer to the sinking liner told of hearing the strains of 'Nearer, My God, to Thee.'" Mowbray then wrote, "The serene strains of the hymn and the frantic cries of the dying blended in a symphony of sorrow." Those who were going to live and those who were going to die were comforted by this hymn. Surely, the wandering spirit of Sarah Adams heard the hymn she had written when she was facing her own personal crisis.

As electric power began to fade, the *Titanic*'s lights turned a dull red, and Father Thomas Byles led the faithful in saying:

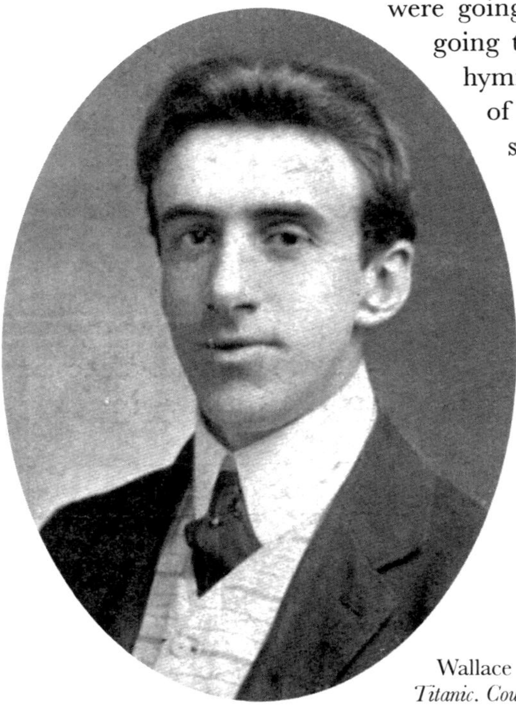

Wallace Hartley, who led the musicians on the *Titanic*. *Courtesy of Wikimedia Commons.*

Ave Maria, gratia plena,
Dominus tecum,
Benedicta tu in mulieribus,
Et benedictus fructus ventris tui, Jesus.
Sancta Maria, Mater Dei,
Ora pro nobis peccatoribus, nunc, et in hora mortis nostrae.
Amen.

And the Jewish passengers surely repeated these ancient words: "Hear O Israel: the Lord is our God, the Lord is One."

The *Titanic*'s stern rose higher and higher, exposing her three massive propellers. As the stern continued to rise even higher, people lost their grip on the rails and slid screaming into the freezing ocean; dishes crashed to the floor; heavy equipment broke loose; a funnel crashed into the sea, crushing those that it hit; and dogs began to swim away from the dying ship. Even the rats were seeking to survive. Suddenly, there was a mighty roar, and the ship, already half submerged, was seen to buckle and apparently break in two. Twenty seconds after starting her death plunge, the *Titanic* entered her watery grave, soon to be joined by over 1,500 people who had planned a trip to the New World. It was said that Captain Smith's last command to his crew was the admonition to "Be British."

Lady Duff Gordon wrote, "The boat stood like an enormous black finger against the sky. Little figures hung and dropped into the water. The screaming was agonizing. I never heard such a chorus of utter despair and agony." Those in the lifeboats had witnessed the deaths of over 1,500 people. But death did not come easy for those left floating in the icy water. They screamed, yelled and prayed until death's angel mercifully brought them peace. The ship that some thought to be unsinkable had passed into history. Many decades would pass before it would be seen again.

As the *Titanic* died and the music stopped, those who could not get into a lifeboat were dead within twenty minutes due to the icy water. Some swimmers got to a lifeboat and were pulled aboard, but most were held above water in their life jackets as they froze to death. The life jackets that were designed to save lives only prolonged a horrible death. What were their last thoughts as their lives faded away?

A number of men—including Colonel Archibald Gracie, Second Officer Charles Lightoller, Jack Thayer and Robert Daniel—were saved by jumping into the water and being picked up by lifeboats. These men were rarely criticized since they saved themselves after the ship was lost. They did not deprive a woman or a child of a place in a lifeboat. Robert Daniel was from Philadelphia, but he had strong Richmond connections. His survival would become major news in Richmond.

Those men who were picked up by a lifeboat were very fortunate since many people refused to aid those in the freezing water. Although there were many vacant seats in the lifeboats, only one lifeboat returned to the *Titanic*'s grave to pick up those freezing in the water. The reason given for not returning was the fear that those in the water might grab and overturn the lifeboats. And there has been some speculation that some of the women did not want to return to save their husbands freezing in the ocean, because they were in unhappy marriages and they would be better off if their husbands were dead. Divorce was a stigma for a woman, but to lose one's husband in a disaster was quite acceptable and, for some women, quite fortunate.

Within a few minutes, over 1,500 people were dead, while 706 were still waiting in lifeboats to be rescued. The lifeboats had to be rowed through a sea of the dead as the oars splashed into the water and struck floating bodies.

The silent sea claimed its dead as stars twinkled overhead. One passenger commented that she had never seen so many shooting stars and then recalled an old story that whenever there was a shooting star, someone would die. With so many dead, the sky must have been ablaze with shooting stars. Now the survivors could only pray and strain their eyes to see the red and green lights of the speeding *Carpathia*.

As they waited, some people prayed the Lord's Prayer, and Fourth Officer Boxhall lit green flares that arched into the air from his lifeboat. Margaret Brown in boat No. 6 virtually took command of that lifeboat and threatened to knock a crewman overboard. For her leadership, she became known as the "Unsinkable Molly Brown" after quipping, "They can sink, but I can't; I'm unsinkable." In lifeboat No. 1 were Sir Cosmos and Lady Duff Gordon. When crew members in the lifeboat talked about losing their "kits," Sir Cosmos responded, "You need not worry about that: I will give you a fiver each to start a new kit." This offer had two interpretations. One was that it was a pure act of kindness; the other was that it was a bribe to keep the crewmen from returning to the sinking *Titanic* to try to save those in the water. If it was an act of generosity, it was not understood by most people that way. The general conclusion was that it was a bribe for which Sir Cosmos paid with a tainted reputation.

In the lifeboats, there were acts of kindness and there were acts of arrogance and rudeness. Some people shared their warm clothing with others, while one woman complained that a crewman was smoking. One man had a pistol in his pocket and planned to shoot himself and his wife if the situation deteriorated. Some of the survivors were standing on upside-down lifeboats or struggling to stay in water-filled lifeboats. Only good seamanship—and perhaps luck—saved many of those in the lifeboats. Under a magnificent starlit sky, the eyes of the survivors looked for a ship on the horizon—a ship that would save them from a watery grave. Even as they stared into the darkness, the same darkness that the lookouts on the *Titanic* had glared into, they could only see more darkness. But there was hope—and then there was light!

Chapter 9

RMS *Carpathia*

Only a few you see.
May tell the story
Of this great calamity;
Husbands, Wives, perhaps in glory
View the sad catastrophe
The Carpathia *eastern bound*
For the Mediterranean Sea;
Turned to the mighty sound,
The wireless C.Q.D.
—J.H. McKenzie

The rescue vessel that was destined to save those who were able to get into lifeboats or otherwise able to stay alive was the RMS *Carpathia*. This ship had made her maiden voyage for the Cunard Line in 1903 from Liverpool to Boston. The *Carpathia* was much smaller and far less magnificent than the *Titanic*, but now she was the only hope left for the *Titanic*'s survivors. Richmonders would have known about this ship since there were frequent notices in the local newspapers advertising tickets for cruises to Italy and the Mediterranean.

As the *Carpathia* raced to the *Titanic*'s rescue, Captain Rostron demonstrated excellent leadership skills. He quickly gave the orders to prepare the ship for a rescue operation. Once he had given the necessary orders, Captain Rostron was heard saying the Twenty-third Psalm while standing on the bridge

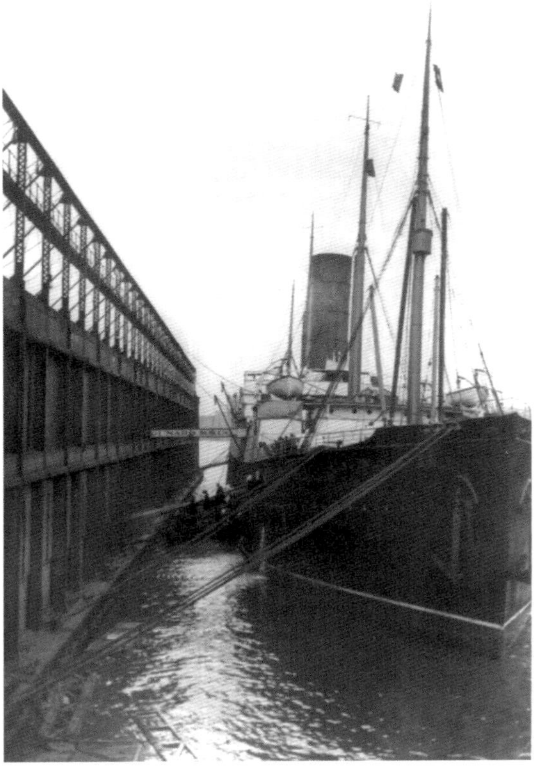

The Cunard liner RMS *Carpathia*. *Courtesy of the Library of Congress.*

as his ship was speeding through dangerous ice-filled waters. He would later say that God must have been steering the ship after seeing all the icebergs that he had managed to avoid in a frantic race to save those who were shivering and dying in lifeboats.

At 3:30 a.m., rockets from the *Carpathia* were sighted by those in the lifeboats, and the crew of the *Carpathia* could see the flares being fired from the lifeboats. When Captain Rostron saw one of the flares floating across the dark sky, he knew he had found the survivors of the *Titanic*, but the *Titanic* was gone. Floating deck chairs and bodies marked her grave. As the *Carpathia* approached the lifeboats, Captain Rostron ordered the engines stopped as he prepared to take on board the *Titanic*'s survivors.

But this was not an easy task. The lifeboats were scattered over a wide area since they had tried to pull away from the *Titanic* for fear that the suction of the ship going down would pull down the lifeboats. As the lifeboats reached the *Carpathia*, several methods were used to get the survivors on board. Those who were able climbed up a rope ladder, which was no easy task. Others were hauled up in a "bosun's chair" or in a canvas bag. Children were brought on board in mail sacks.

At 4:10 a.m., the first lifeboat was picked up, and the work of rescue was completed by 8:10 a.m. As survivors boarded the *Carpathia*, they frantically looked for loved ones who might have been in another lifeboat. Their desperate searches generally ended in floods of tears. Many survivors were overwhelmed by grief as they were aided by both the crew members and passengers on the

Carpathia. One man was helped in an unusual way. He was so cold that he was put in an oven to warm up. Although the *Carpathia* managed to rescue 706 people, over 1,500 were left to float lifeless in life jackets.

By 8:50 a.m., the *Carpathia* was heading west to New York carrying those who had escaped death in the Atlantic Ocean. Other ships would look for survivors but with no success. When the *Carpathia* passed over the grave of the *Titanic* and its lost souls, Captain Rostron conducted a brief memorial service.

As they sailed toward a safe harbor, several people who had been rescued died on the *Carpathia.* Their bodies were sewn in sacks and committed to the deep. An Episcopal priest read these words: "We therefore commit his/her body to the deep, to be turned into corruption, looking for the resurrection of the body, when the sea shall give up her dead, the life of the world to come through our Lord Jesus Christ; who at his coming shall change our vile body, that it may be like his glorious body, according to the mighty working, whereby he is able to subdue all things to himself."

Surviving the sinking of the *Titanic* could have been dependent on what class ticket you held. The following is a tabulation by Greg Ward of those who survived and those who died based on the class for which they held tickets:

FIRST CLASS
32.9 percent of the men survived
97 percent of the women survived
85.7 percent of the children survived

SECOND CLASS
9.4 percent of the men survived
76.9 percent of the women survived
100 percent of the children survived

THIRD CLASS
15.8 percent of the men survived
45.7 percent of the women survived
36.0 percent of the children survived

In summary, 20.2 percent of the men survived, and 73.0 percent of all women survived. Only 23.6 percent of the crew survived. The obvious low survival rate in third class remains a matter of conjecture. Reasons range from third-class passengers being locked below to not being able to find the lifeboats to simply getting lost in the maze of passageways.

There were even some accounts that some third-class passengers rushed the lifeboats and were shot. Mowbray, for example, wrote: "Steerage [third-class] fought their way to the upper decks and struggled with brutal ferocity against cabin passengers who were trying to save themselves. Officers of the ship shot down men who sought to jump into already overcrowded boats. The sounds of the pistol shots mingled with the strains of 'Nearer, My God, to Thee.'" This probably did not happen. But it is obvious that if you were in first class or second class, you had a better chance of survival.

Now was a time of reflection of all the things that could have saved the *Titanic* from disaster. The list is long and some of them might not have saved the ship, but these were the things in the public mind:

- If the watertight door had been one deck higher, the *Titanic* would not have sunk.
- If the *Titanic* had carried sufficient lifeboats, most of the passengers and crew members might have survived.
- If the *Olympic* had not had a collision with the HMS *Hawke*, *Titanic*'s departure would not have been delayed and she would have missed the iceberg.
- If the *Titanic* had collided with the *New York*, the sailing would have been delayed and she would have missed the iceberg.
- If the *Titanic* had heeded the numerous warnings about the iceberg, she might have been saved.
- If there had been waves that would have struck the iceberg, the iceberg would have been more visible to the two lookouts.
- If the moon had been shining, the lookouts might have spotted the iceberg in time.
- If the lookouts had seen the iceberg ten seconds sooner or ten seconds later, the *Titanic* would have missed it or crashed into it. In either case, the *Titanic* would not have sunk.
- If the lookouts had not seen the iceberg, the ship would have hit it head on and survived.
- If the men in the crow's nest had had binoculars, they might have seen the iceberg in time.
- If the abandon ship order had come sooner, more people could have been saved.
- If the lifeboats had been filled to capacity, more people would have been saved.

- If the *Californian* had responded to the many distress calls, more people might have been saved.
- If the *Titanic*'s rudder had been larger, it might have been able to turn the *Titanic* in time.
- If the *Titanic* had been thirty feet longer or shorter, she would have missed the iceberg.
- If the Atlantic had not been overly warm, the iceberg would not have formed.
- If Murdoch had not tried to navigate around the iceberg but had hit it, the *Titanic* would not have sunk.

As the *Carpathia* steamed toward New York City, there was almost a news blackout except for the fact that the *Titanic* had sunk with the loss of many lives. The only significant communications from the *Carpathia* were the names of the survivors; it provided virtually no other news about the sinking of the *Titanic* to an anxiously waiting world. This news blackout continued until the *Carpathia* docked and the passengers and crew could be interviewed by the media. The survivors, who began their voyage in a ship built for luxury, ended up on a ship that many of the elite passengers would have viewed with disdain. They were used to better accommodations, but the *Carpathia* had arrived safely, while the *Titanic* was being explored by fish in its watery grave.

Chapter 10

Richmonders Read About a Collision at Sea

It was on one Monday morning
Just about one o'clock
When the great ship Titanic
Began to reel and rock
People began to scream and cry
Saying Lord I'm a-gonna die
It was sad when that great ship went down
—William and Versey Smith

In 1912, the population of Richmond was about 130,000. Having recovered from the Civil War, the city was beginning to thrive. It was known for its production of tobacco products, paper and fertilizer. There were also granite quarries and flour mills. New high-rise buildings were being constructed along Main Street, and public transportation was available on streetcars. Along Monument Avenue, monuments to Confederate leaders were being dedicated and Confederate reunions were held on a regular basis. A writer summarized the city in 1912 as a place where "business buzzes, traffic roars, sky-scrapers soar to heaven, and numberless smokestacks proclaim that everything in the world, from matches to locomotives, is made in Richmond."

Richmond increased in size in 1910 when it annexed Manchester, and to facilitate travel across the James River, the Mayo Bridge was built. Richmond also had a new city hall, a public auditorium and many churches. Indeed,

Richmond was known as a churchgoing community. But Richmond was not known for its racial tolerance. There was strict segregation and an occasional boycott by African Americans in a quest for equality.

To accommodate a growing population, more apartments were being built, as were more private homes. One characteristic of the new homes was a brass knocker on the front door. Streets were generally of cobblestone and traversed by both horse-drawn carriages and Model T Fords. Richmonders were buying Daisy Bread, Airfloat talcum powder and ostrich feathers. Richmond was a rapidly growing southern city.

The major news story in April 1912 that attracted the attention of Richmonders was the Hillsville Massacre in Carroll County, Virginia. In a courthouse shootout, the Allen clan killed the judge, the sheriff, the commonwealth's attorney, a juror and a spectator and injured several other people. But the shootout was driven off the front pages by the *Titanic* disaster. For the rest of April, the story of the *Titanic* would unfold day by day, providing Richmonders and the rest of the world with ever-increasing information about the tragedy.

Today we get news almost as it happens. Disasters are immediately reported on television and radio, in newspapers, on the Internet and through a host of electronic devices. In 1912, however, Richmonders got their news from the local newspapers: the *Times Dispatch*, *News Leader*, *Richmond Planet* and *Evening Journal*. Breaking news of importance was published in "Extra Editions," which were sold on street corners by young boys.

The newspapers got their local news from reporters, and the other news, such as the sinking of the *Titanic*, was received by wireless telegraph using Morse code. But the ability to communicate a clear message by Morse code was dependent on a number of factors, including the skill of the operator, the time of day and the weather conditions. And there was always the real possibility of a misunderstanding because of a signal distortion of a message sent over long distances. In essence, there was a chance that what was communicated from the *Carpathia* and other ships was not always understood and transcribed correctly. Because of these variables and perhaps some unfortunate guessing, the first news of the sinking *Titanic* was reported in the newspapers with various elements of truth and fiction. It has been suggested that in the absence of news from the *Carpathia*, some newspaper editors simply filled in the blanks with their best guesses.

On the front page of the *Times Dispatch* for April 15 was this brief headline: "*Titanic* Reported to Have Struck Iceberg." And the following story read, "Montreal, Quebec, April 14—The new White Star liner *Titanic* is reported

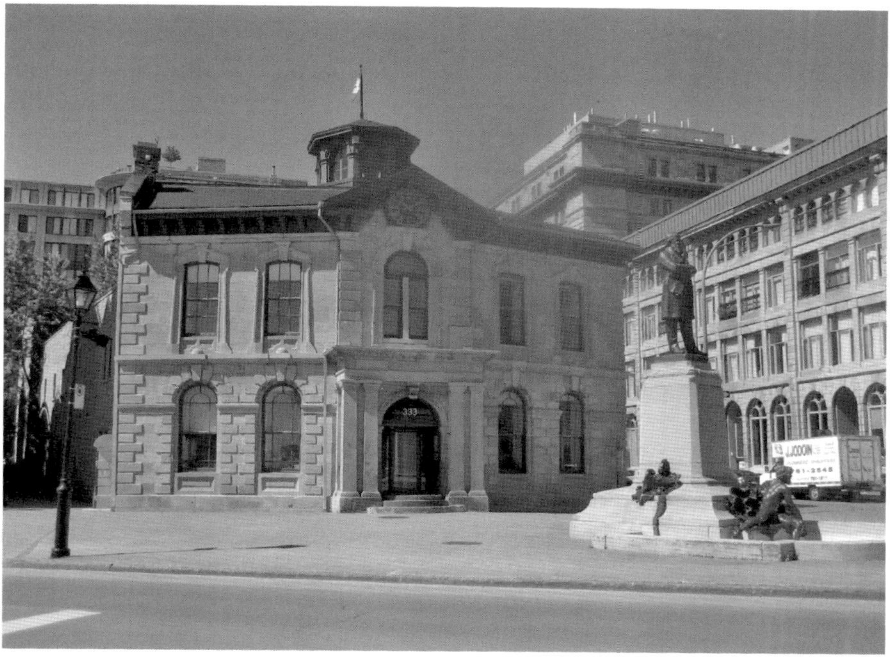

The Allan Building in Montreal where the message was received that the *Titanic* had hit an iceberg. *Photograph by Cara F. Griggs.*

in advices received here late to-night to have struck an iceberg. The SS *Viginian* reported that she was on her way to the *Titanic*."

This headline was based on a wireless received from the *Titanic* sent at 12:40 a.m. on April 15 that was picked up at the wireless station at Cape Race and by the Allen Company's ship *Virginian*, which then wired the information to its home office in Montreal, Quebec. Upon receipt of the information in Montreal, the Montreal wireless office wired it to the newspapers, and it was picked up at the wireless office at the *Times Dispatch* building at No. 4 North Tenth Street in Richmond. The *Times Dispatch* only reported the known facts and nothing else.

Unlike the *Times Dispatch*, the *Evening Journal*, a newspaper distributed in Richmond, yielded to speculation and sensationalism. If you picked up that newspaper, you would have read a headline that proclaimed that all had been saved from the *Titanic*. The newspaper reported that those on the *Titanic* had been "transferred to other ships that came up." In an expansion of the headline, there was a story that the "Cunard liner *Carpathia*, called by an aerial flash asking for aid, rushed to the assistance of the giant liner *Titanic* in the darkness off Newfoundland today [April 15, 1912] and took on board 1,300 passengers from the great vessel which had struck an iceberg late last night on her maiden voyage to New York." The article even explained that passengers were taken off the *Titanic* in small boats and transferred to the *Carpathia*. It was also reported that the *Titanic* was low in the water but was headed to Halifax for repairs. It is almost incomprehensible how such a work of fiction could have been written as breaking news, but it was what some Richmonders read. The next day, the newspaper reported that the false report was attributed "to amateurs who sent out reports that the passengers of the *Titanic* had all been saved." In essence, the claim was made that the wireless had been tampered with by some amateurs, which resulted in false information being printed.

Other newspapers published both similar and very different stories. The *New York Times* took a chance and published this headline: "New Liner *Titanic* Hits an Iceberg; Sinking by the Bow at Midnight; Women Put Off in Lifeboats; Latest Wireless at 12:27 a.m. Blurred." The publisher could not prove all of these statements, but he went with his gut feeling and made journalism history for being right. A Minnesota newspaper reported that the *Titanic* had hit an iceberg and was reported to be sinking. The *Evening World* in Roanoke, Virginia, reported the story with this headline: "*Titanic* Crushed by Iceberg. Mighty Steamer on the Brink of Ruin."

However, many newspapers got the story wrong and raised hopes that would soon be dashed. The *New York World* reported as follows: "The Disabled Ship Under Tow After Hitting Big Iceberg." The *Chicago Day Book* reported: "Liner *Titanic* Wrecked by Iceberg: Passengers Transferred to Other Vessels in Mid-Ocean." The *Hawaiian Star* carried a brief story that reported that the "passengers on the *Titanic* [were] rescued and the ship was sinking." The *Evening Standard* published in Ogden, Utah, reported: "Passengers from the *Titanic* Rescued." The *Seattle Star* reported: "*Titanic* Hits Iceberg: People Safe." The *Christian Science Monitor* reported: "Passengers Safely Moved and *Titanic* Taken in Tow." The *Washington Times* reported: "Liner *Titanic* Kept Afloat by Water-Tight Compartments Being Towed into Halifax, Nova Scotia." The *Daily Mail* in London reported: "The *Titanic* Sunk, No Lives Lost."

Since there were numerous reports that the *Titanic* was under tow, it was reported that there was no dock in America large enough to accommodate and repair the *Titanic*. The *Times Dispatch* also quoted a White Star Line official as follows: "We are perfectly satisfied that the *Titanic* is unsinkable. We are absolutely certain that she is able to withstand any damages. She may be down by the head, but would float indefinitely in that condition." Perhaps some editors really believed the *Titanic* was unsinkable and allowed this belief to fill in the gaps in their coverage.

The *News Leader*, Richmond's evening newspaper, reported in large type on April 15: "Atlantic Leviathan in Collision with Iceberg." It was also reported that "all passengers had been saved and the *Titanic* was still afloat but in sinking condition." In addition to focusing on the disaster, the newspaper reported that Robert W. Daniel, a former Richmonder, was on the *Titanic* and that his mother lived in Richmond. The focus on Robert Daniel included the fact that he was born in Richmond and was a descendant of a distinguished family. He was a graduate of the University of Virginia, a star athlete, a former employee of the Richmond Fredericksburg and Potomac Railroad and an insurance and bank executive. He had relocated to Philadelphia at the time of the *Titanic* disaster.

The same newspaper reported that ships had recently reported icebergs in the area where the *Titanic* had met her fate and that there were not enough lifeboats to save everyone. By the end of the day, Richmonders knew there had been a major disaster at sea and that many people had perished. Soon, Richmonders would be overwhelmed with information about the *Titanic*—information that was difficult to comprehend. It is still difficult to comprehend today.

Richmonders did not learn the story all at once but little by little as new information was published in the newspapers. In the days ahead, the story of the tragedy would be revealed as it became available. Some days there was new information, and some days there was nothing new to report. People wanted to know the whole story at one time, but this did not happen. Today we would know the story in real time, but real time did not exist in 1912.

Chapter 11

Tuesday, April 16, 1912

> Titanic *was the ship just on her maiden trip,*
> *To sail across the Atlantic Ocean wide;*
> *It was a pleasure trip—millionaires aboard the ship,*
> *But they never lived to reach the other side.*
> *—Richard D. Burnett*

The *Times Dispatch* had excellent first-page coverage of the *Titanic* disaster on April 16. Readers saw a beautiful picture of the magnificent ship, and there was the following headline: "*Titanic*, Giant White Star Liner, Sinks After Collision with Iceberg on Her Maiden Voyage, and 1,800 Lives Are Reported Lost in World's Greatest Marine Disaster." The entire front page was filled with various stories about the catastrophe and the incomprehensible loss of life.

Richmonders read about the heroic deaths of the wealthy men on board, including John Jacob Astor, and the survival of his young bride; the deaths of many other well-known people; and the financial blow to the White Star Line. But little coverage was given to what may be described as "ordinary passengers."

For many Richmonders, the main story was in an article entitled "Richmond People on the *Titanic*." The main focus was Robert Daniel. He had the closest Richmond connection of any of the survivors. Because many Richmonders knew him or his family, there was a great deal of interest in his fate. There were unconfirmed reports that he might have survived.

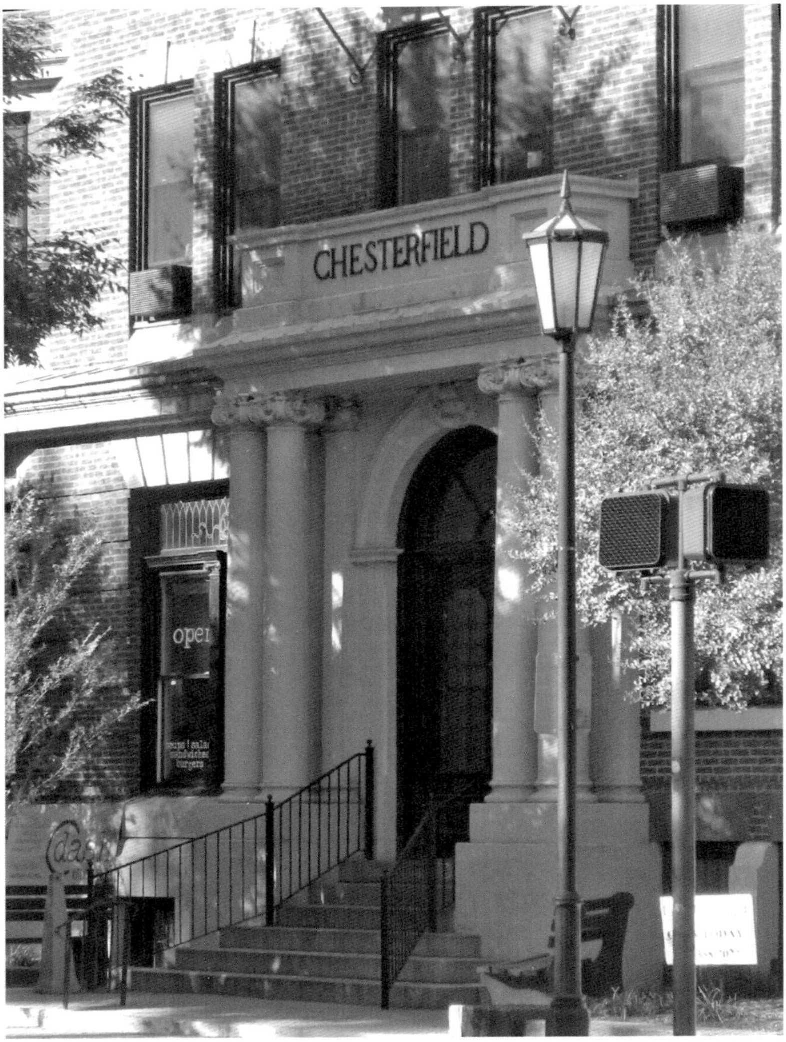

Chesterfield Apartment Building in Richmond where the mother of Robert Daniel lived in 1912. *Photograph by Walter S. Griggs.*

His mother, who lived in the Chesterfield Apartments on Franklin Street in Richmond, could only wait for news of her son.

Jacques Futrelle and his wife, May, also had ties to Richmond. He was a former reporter for the *Richmond Times*, and his wife had been an actress at the local Bijou Theater. Richmonders were anxious to find out if they had been rescued. Mrs. Moses Thalhimer of Richmond reported that her first and second cousins Mrs. L.D. Greenfield and her son W.D. Greenfield had been saved. Both of the cousins lived in New York City, and Mrs. Thalhimer learned of their rescue after telegraphing a friend there. In the next few days, more people with Richmond connections would be mentioned in the newspaper.

In the absence of news from the *Carpathia* regarding the *Titanic*, the newspaper published articles on ocean liners basically to fill up pages. There was an interview concerning the possibility of building an unsinkable ship. At the time of the interview, those being interviewed knew the *Titanic* had struck an iceberg, but they did not know her fate. One of the men interviewed was Rear Admiral David W. Taylor of Louisa County, Virginia. The admiral commented, "No amount of scientific shipbuilding would probably save a ship should she strike a berg hard enough." He then offered the suggestion that the fate of the *Titanic* would settle the question within the next twelve hours as to whether an unsinkable ship could be built.

While people were reading about the sinking of the *Titanic*, the *Carpathia* was heading to New York. She was avoiding icebergs and caring for those who had survived the disaster but still not providing any news except for the names of survivors, which were sometimes garbled in transmission. Even a request from President William Howard Taft for information on his military aide, Major Archibald Butt, was not answered. The waiting world wanted to know what had happened, but only the names of survivors were being reported.

People whose loved ones' names were not transmitted by the *Carpathia* were grasping at any possibility that they might be on other ships that had raced to the site of the sinking of the *Titanic*. Both the *Parisian* and *Virginian* were known to have been near the *Titanic* and might have picked up some survivors without reporting that they were on board. Families were grabbing at anything that might give hope that a loved one had survived.

The Richmond newspapers began to be philosophical. Richmonders read in the newspaper, "The last words of science, art, and limitless resources were spoken in the construction and equipment of this great floating palace; but in conflict with natural forces, it shattered like a cockleshell, and its immensity served merely to measure the extent of the calamity of its loss. Thus it is that the forces of nature caused the most ambitious work of men—the most splendid triumph of science and art—to look mean and petty." The newspaper tried to be optimistic with the comment: "Let us earnestly trust that the extent of this calamity may not be so great as it at present appears."

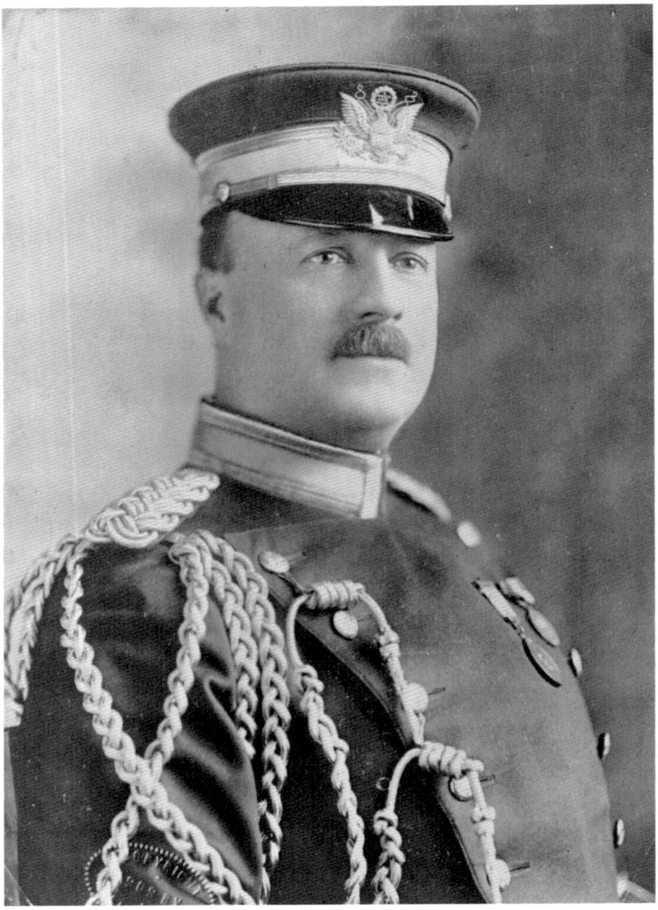

Major Archibald Butt, the military advisor to President William Howard Taft. *Courtesy of the Library of Congress.*

In an editorial in the Richmond evening newspaper, the writer commented: "Unspeakable horror spread over the world yesterday as it learned of the sinking of the *Titanic*. The gruesome story pales the imagination and every hour brings more sickening intelligence. The largest vessel ever built, the masterpiece of man's constructive genius freighted with an army of precious human lives, vanished in an instant. When heaven was all tranquility, death's dark reef lay straight ahead."

Still looking for added news, the newspaper again commented on the size of the *Titanic*. To make the sheer size of the *Titanic* real to Richmonders, the newspaper printed a picture showing the height of the *Titanic* compared to famous buildings. In the comparison, the *Titanic* was taller than the Bunker Hill Monument, the Washington Monument, the Pyramids of Egypt and St. Peter's Cathedral in Rome.

Like the morning newspaper, the *News Leader* provided some editorial comments. The writer commented, "Men stand appalled in the face of so frightful a disaster as the sinking of the *Titanic*." The *Evening Journal* in an editorial suggested the cause of the disaster in the following paragraph: "Perhaps racing at top speed on her maiden voyage to make a record that should establish the reputation of the ship in the eyes of the public, this great bulk of steel, weighing 66,000 tons, plunged into a mountainous iceberg, and though built to sustain shocks and to float with portions of her hull wrecked, she crumpled and bent like cardboard in the tremendous impact with an immovable object, and perhaps, went down in less time than reported."

The day ended with Richmonders knowing one piece of good news. It was reported that Mrs. Daniel had heard that her son, Robert Daniel, was safe and on board the *Carpathia*; however, his champion French bulldog, Gamin de Pycombe, did not survive. In the days ahead, there would be many more stories about the rescue of Robert Daniel.

Chapter 12
Wednesday, April 17, 1912

As the moon rose in its glory,
And it drifted to the golden west;
It told a sad new story,
Sixteen hundred had gone to rest.
—*author unknown*

Richmonders who read the morning newspaper on April 17 saw a long list of those who were reported lost on the *Titanic*. Not on the list was the president of the White State Line, J. Bruce Ismay. In the days ahead, his absence from the list would become a major news story.

There were many comments that men who were "masters of millions stood aside while boats were filled with women and children." There were repeated stories of brave men who died so women and children could live. But blame also started to be placed. Initially, it was placed on Captain Edward J. Smith, who was referred to as the "Sea's Grand Old Man" and the "millionaires' captain" since millionaires liked to travel on ships he commanded.

There was also a major story about Jacques Futrelle, a former reporter who once worked in Richmond. The *Times Dispatch* reported that he had drowned but that his wife, May, had been saved. The newspaper reported, "He had many friends in Richmond where for several years he had served as a news writer for the *Richmond Times*, now the *Times Dispatch*." Readers were reminded that he had had several articles published in the Richmond newspaper in recent months. Although the article reported that he had died, another article carried an unverified report that he might have been rescued. As in most cases, these reports were wishful thinking.

The newspaper continued to report that Robert Daniel had survived. The *Evening Journal* reported as follows: "As the survivors' list was read, the names were ticked off alphabetically–first the A's, then the B's and C's until the D's were reached—there was awful suspense among the reporters gathered about the receiving operator. Great was the rejoicing when the operator ticked off as the first of the D's—D-A-N-I-E-L—followed by the initials R.W." This news was telephoned to his mother by one of the *Journal* men, who had just talked to her at her apartment, where she had spent a sleepless night near the telephone.

In addition, there was published an expanded list of Richmonders who had connections with those on the *Titanic*. First Officer Murdoch, who was in command of the *Titanic* when she struck the iceberg, had a cousin, James T. Sloan, who lived in Richmond. Miss Marie Young, who was reported as having survived, had relatives in Richmond, but her home was in New York City. Miss Young had visited Richmond several times and was an attendant at a Richmond wedding. And there was a comment about Mrs. Bradley Johnston, who had booked passage on the *Titanic* for its return trip to Europe. Obviously, she would not make the trip.

The massive size of the *Titanic* was once again illustrated for Richmonders. It was pointed out that if the *Titanic* was placed on her keel, she would have reached from the *Times Dispatch* building on Main Street to the Virginia Railway and Power Company's building on Seventh Street. It was also noted that "the size of her crew alone would exceed the population of Ashland, Virginia, and the crew and passengers together would exceed the population of Blackstone, Virginia."

In the absence of any news from the *Carpathia*, the newspapers once again filled their pages with stories speculating on how the *Titanic* might have been destroyed. One such report in the Richmond newspaper stated:

> *When the* Titanic *struck* [the iceberg], *she struck hard. There was something more than a rending and tearing of bow plates and a flooding of a few forward compartments. As the whispering of the wireless was pieced together, the* Titanic *must have recoiled from her destroyer a shattered and riven ship. So tremendous an impact would shake the mighty engines from their foundations, open up watertight compartments, buckle plates from end to end, and strew rivets everywhere. It is likely that water rushed into her hull from all sides, for her keel must have been injured by the terrific drive*

> *on a mass as hard as rock. And that jar must have quenched the ship's lights by injuring her electrical apparatus.*

Although subsequent events would refute most of this analysis, it did give Richmonders something to read about in the absence of any news from the *Carpathia.*

With such a frightful loss of life, there were those who believed that people would no longer risk their lives on ocean liners. This was not the case in Richmond. It was reported by several travel agencies that Richmonders who had booked passage on the *Titanic* called the travel agents and "readily consented to transfer to other steamers." S.H. Bowman, a local travel agent, said that he had not had a single passenger "abandon travel" because of the *Titanic.* He also said that the loss of the *Titanic* would result in "future safeguards that will be thrown about ocean travel, and that it will be even safer than it has been heretofore." C.O. Alley, another Richmond travel agent, said, "I have been busy all day in making arrangement for booking *Titanic* passengers to other ships."

There were many editorials. One editorial writer observed: "What a mockery was the name *Titanic*. There was nothing titanic in her save a lust for size, for speed, for luxurious splendor...She was a show-ship, a defiance and cockleshell when the icy peril that dwells in the deep thrusts its relentless fingers through her paper sides and the old ocean sucked her down among its quiet forests, two miles beyond the sight of man, forever. And there like a broken toy, crumpled and tossed aside, she will rest, while the sightless monsters and the tiny life of submarine silences flit through the tapestried saloon and inland parlors." The writer did praise those who stepped aside so women and children could be saved, and it was pointed out that "God seems near at hand when such a disaster occurs."

Even before the *Carpathia* arrived and the full story was revealed, the United States Senate took action and passed Senate Resolution 283. Although not reported until the next day, this resolution charged a committee headed by William Alden Smith of Michigan to "investigate the cause leading to the wreck of the White Star liner *Titanic*, with its attendant loss of life so shocking to the civilized world." The resolution empowered the committee "to summon witnesses, to determine the responsibility of the disaster, to suggest ways to prevent another such disaster and to propose such legislation that the committee might deem appropriate." Before it completed its work, this committee would examine over eighty-two witnesses and publish 1,100 pages of testimony.

In the days ahead, this committee's interviews would provide startling revelations and daily news stories.

The same newspaper reported that the French liner *France* was preparing to make her maiden voyage from France to America. The *France* had four stacks like the *Titanic*, and it was a luxurious ship, destined for a long career. And like the *Titanic*, she carried a number of distinguished passengers. It must

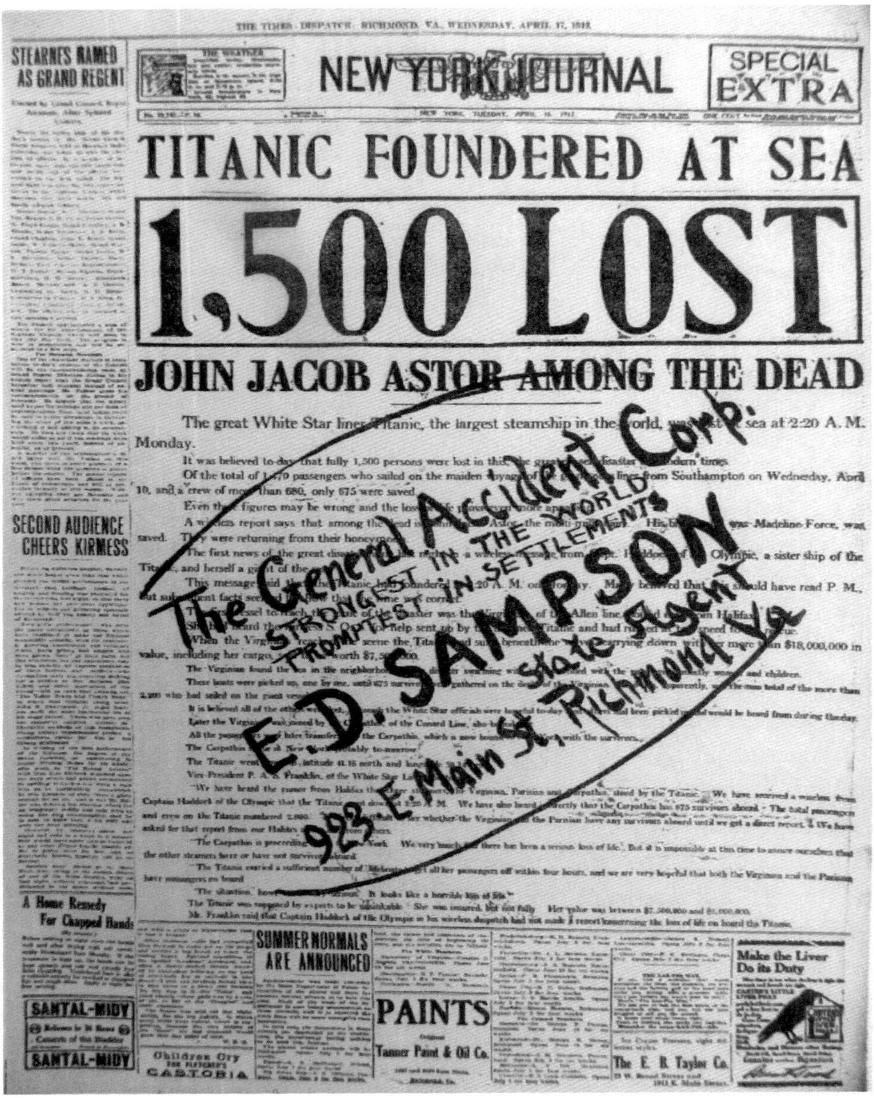

STEARNES NAMED AS GRAND REGENT

NEW YORK JOURNAL

SPECIAL EXTRA

TITANIC FOUNDERED AT SEA

1,500 LOST

JOHN JACOB ASTOR AMONG THE DEAD

The great White Star liner Titanic, the largest steamship in the world, [illegible] sea at 2:20 A. M. Monday.

It was believed to-day that fully 1,500 persons were lost in this, [illegible] disaster [illegible] modern times.

Of the total of [illegible] passengers who sailed on the maiden voyage [illegible] from Southampton on Wednesday, April 10, and a crew of more than 680, only 675 were saved.

Even these figures may be wrong and the loss [illegible]

A wireless report says that among the dead is [illegible] Astor, the multi-millionaire. His [illegible] was Madeline Force, was saved. They were returning from their honeymoon.

The first news of the great disaster [illegible] a wireless message from Capt. Haddock of the Olympic, a sister ship of the Titanic, and herself a giant of the [illegible]

This message said that the Titanic had foundered [illegible] 2:20 A. M. on Monday. Many believed that this should have read P. M., but subsequent facts seemed to show that the time was correct.

[illegible] Allen line [illegible] from Halifax [illegible]

[illegible] Titanic and had rushed at top speed to the rescue.

When the Virginian reached the scene the Titanic had sunk beneath the waves carrying down with her more than $18,000,000 in value, including her cargo, [illegible] worth $7,500,000.

[illegible]

SECOND AUDIENCE CHEERS KIRMESS

A Home Remedy For Chapped Hands

SUMMER NORMALS ARE ANNOUNCED

PAINTS

Tanner Paint & Oil Co.

Make the Liver Do its Duty

The E. B. Taylor Co.

SANTAL-MIDY

SANTAL-MIDY

Children Cry FOR FLETCHER'S CASTORIA

The General Accident Corp.

STRONGEST IN THE WORLD

PROMPTEST IN SETTLEMENTS

E. D. SAMPSON

State Agent

923 E. Main St., Richmond Va.

Life insurance advertisement that was in the *Times Dispatch*. *Author's collection.*

have taken some special kind of courage to get on a ship to sail essentially the same route that had sent the *Titanic* to the bottom. Fortunately, history did not repeat itself.

Even though the world was wrapped in grief, there were some who took advantage of the disaster to sell their products. One advertisement had a picture of a newspaper article concerning the number of lives lost on the ship, and in handwriting across the headline was the following advertisement: "The General Accident Corp, E.D. Sampson, State Agent, 923 E. Main St, Richmond, Va." This company provided insurance, which would have certainly helped the families of those lost on the *Titanic*. But there might be some question about taking advantage of a tragedy to sell a product.

There was another story that also seemed out of place. While the world mourned the death of so many, baseball great Ty Cobb of the Detroit Tigers was throwing a temper tantrum in Chicago. His room in the Chicago Beach Hotel was next to the railroad tracks. When the noise of the trains disturbed him, he insisted on a different room. When his request was denied, it was reported, "Tyrus refused to play in the afternoon game against the White Sox, and in the evening he packed his trunk and took the train back to Detroit." His thoughts about the tragedy of the *Titanic* are unknown.

And so the day ended!

Chapter 13

Thursday, April 18, 1912

Be British! The captain cried out from the bridge,
Be British and British they were,
The women, the children for the boats,
And the sailors knew how to obey,
As long as old England sends ships over sea,
The deeds of that night she'll recall,
When rich man and poor man went down side by side,
When rank made no difference for Death leveled all.
—F.V. St. Clair

In the days before sophisticated communication, the news of the *Carpathia*'s arrival in New York on April 18 was not reported in either the morning or evening newspapers. Instead, the *Times Dispatch* still carried headlines filled with frustration. For example, "*Carpathia* Refuses to Give Any Details of *Titanic*'s Loss and As Fruitless Hours Go By, Suspense Grows More Maddening." The newspaper reported that there was no new news, but that in a few hours, the truth would be known when the *Carpathia* docked in New York and the full story of the loss of the *Titanic* would be told.

There was a report that the ship SS *Baltic* was bringing 250 survivors to New York, and there was another story that discredited the *Baltic* story. But such rumors of survival must have put families with lost loved ones in a state of constant anxiety ranging from hope to hopelessness.

People were wondering and asking how the president of the White Star Line, J. Bruce Ismay, managed to survive. It was even reported that before he arrived in New York, he would be summoned to appear before the United States Senate Committee. This committee that met at the Waldorf Astoria Hotel in New York City and in Washington, D.C., was waiting for him. On the *Carpathia*, he remained a recluse locked in a cabin, and he was making plans for a quick return to England along with the surviving crew members. This was not to be!

The newspapers also continued to focus on those with some connection to Richmond. H.W. Walthall of East Leigh Street was completing a tour of Europe and had made arrangements to sail home from England on the *Titanic*. At the last minute, he changed his mind and decided to spend more time in London to see more of the city. He probably owed his life to the attractions of London.

News about Jacques Futrelle was again in the newspapers. It was noted that he had had a premonition of death. Before sailing, both he and his wife had sent powers of attorney to administer their estates if anything should happen to them on the voyage. He wrote, "You never know what might happen and you want everything straight for the kiddies." It was reported that Mrs. Daniel had left for New York to meet her son upon his arrival on board the *Carpathia*.

As more news of the *Titanic* became available, Richmonders began writing to the newspaper about the ship. One published letter suggested that "the terrible catastrophe would not have happened had the *Titanic* been running to the Chesapeake Bay instead of New York City." It was felt that a southern port would have avoided icebergs. The letter concluded, "The South needs a port of immigration and immigrants will clamor for a 'safe' route which a direct line to the Chesapeake will provide." If this suggestion had been taken, Norfolk would have become the gateway to America. But it did not happen.

Like the United States, England was struggling with issues surrounding the *Titanic*. One issue was quite unusual. Women in England were seeking the right to vote, so some of the leaders of the suffragettes were asked how they viewed the "women and children first" rule on the *Titanic*. One suffragette admitted that "she admired the men for their heroism, but suggested their heroism should not be placed on too high a plane. It was almost a natural law that women and children should be saved first; the children because childhood is sacred and the women because they are so necessary to the race that they cannot be spared." The suffragette then asserted, "The lives of women are more important to the race than the lives of men." As a final thought, she observed, "Man is chivalrous at moments of a crisis, but in the aggregate the balance of chivalry is on the part of women." It is not known how the men of Richmond responded to this article.

Chapter 14

FRIDAY, APRIL 19, 1912

As the big ship rolled and dipped,
He went to sleep in the mighty deep.
My sweetheart went down with the ship.
—Roger Lewis and F. Henri Klickmann

This was a big news day! The Richmond newspapers could finally report on the arrival of the *Titanic*'s survivors who were aboard the *Carpathia*. Following a voyage in bitterly cold but sunny weather, the *Carpathia* docked in New York City at Pier 54 at 9:26 a.m. on April 18. It was a cool, rainy day, which fit the mood of the thousands waiting to greet the *Titanic* survivors. In the crowd were both family members and anxious reporters. Those on board the *Carpathia* could see that every flag, either on ship or shore, was at half-staff in honor of those who were lost in the disaster. Many of those who had embarked on a voyage in joy and excitement now returned home from the sea without a loved one, filled with grief and with tragic memories of the dead and dying that would never go away. The one scene that seemed out of place was that the Duff Gordons had arranged for a photographer to take a picture of them with their fellow survivors from the lifeboat wearing their life jackets.

The newspaper reported that when the *Carpathia* docked, the survivors were "lifted from the gates of death and were in the arms of their friends." Some of the survivors left immediately. They did not want to relive a tragedy by talking to reporters. A committee of survivors gave the press a copy of the following statement: "We, the undersigned surviving passengers from the steamship *Titanic*, in order to forestall any sensational or exaggerated statements, deem it our duty to give to the press a statement of facts which have come to our knowledge and which we believe to be true." The press was presented with a chronological list of the events. Of course, not all passengers and crew members agreed with this declaration.

Reporters, who swarmed around the passengers, tried many ways to get a story. Methods included having a *Titanic* survivor toss a manuscript to someone on a waiting tugboat, offering money for an exclusive story, listening to gossip, quizzing *Titanic* crew members, asking passengers on the *Carpathia* what they had been told and sneaking on board the *Carpathia*. Generally, the first question that was asked by a reporter was whether the officers shot passengers and themselves. Eventually, the stories were collected and published. Some stories were accurate, and some were filled with fantasy. The readers could not figure out which stories were true and which were false, and some of the erroneous stories are still told and believed today.

The *Times Dispatch* headline was gruesome: "*Titanic*'s Death List, 1,601. Only 739 Lives Are Saved." Another story reported that 745 people had been rescued, but 6 of those had died on board the *Carpathia* and had been buried at sea. One writer made three points for his readers: the death toll was higher than expected, the list of prominent persons who died had not changed and many of the women were saved, except for those who refused to leave their husbands. Subsequent reports would discredit some of these points.

There were many comments about the fate of Captain Smith. One survivor commented that Captain Smith shot himself on the bridge of the ship before it went under. Other passengers said they saw Captain Smith drown. One passenger claimed to have seen Captain Smith put a child in a lifeboat, and then he disappeared from view. It was reported that some passengers were very calm as they waited for a lifeboat, while others suggested there was chaos. Some of these inconsistencies can be explained by overactive imaginations and others by where a person was on the ship when the *Titanic* went down. Due to the size of the ship, a person on the starboard side could see one thing whereas a person on the port side might see something entirely different. It was a matter of location, as well as imagination, that determined the story that was told.

There were many stories in the Richmond newspapers about what the passengers felt when the *Titanic* hit the iceberg. Richmonders read that many passengers did not feel anything, or if they did, it was described as a rather minor vibration or scraping. However, one passenger commented, "I was eating when the boat hit the iceberg. There was an awful shock that made the boat tremble from stem to stern; I did not know what had happened. I felt the boat rise and it seemed to me that she was riding over the ice. I ran out on deck, and then I could see ice. It was a veritable sea of ice, and the boat was rocking over it. I jumped into the ocean and was picked up by one of the lifeboats." Based on known accounts, this one was pure fantasy, but it was what Richmonders read and, perhaps, some believed.

The newspapers were filled with emotional stories from the lost ship. Richmonders were deeply moved when the beautiful love story was shared about how Mrs. Isidor (Ida) Straus refused to leave her husband when he refused to get into a lifeboat before any other man. It was pointed out in the Richmond newspaper that Isidor Straus had been sent abroad by the Confederate government to buy supplies for the Confederacy. At the time of his death, he owned Macy's Department Store in New York City. It was also reported that Colonel John Jacob Astor was a hero because he put his pregnant wife into a lifeboat and then died with the rest of the men after being told that no men could enter a lifeboat until all of the women and children were off the ship.

Because of his connection to Richmond, the story of how Robert Daniel survived was reported over and over again in more detail. Mr. Daniel stated that he was in bed when the ship struck the iceberg. When asked to report what happened to him, he said, "Oh, I can't tell what happened. I hardly know myself. I was naked. I grabbed something and uttered a prayer, then I went over the side of the boat." His additional comments are difficult to put in a logical order. At one point he claimed to have felt "a cake of ice nearby, I clung to it. For five hours I battled with the ice, and when I saw other boats near, I almost gave up." It was also reported that he escaped in one of the *Titanic*'s collapsible lifeboats. Daniel stated that "five minutes after the crash everybody seemed to have gone insane. Men and women fought, bit, and scratched to be in a lifeboat. Look at my black eye and cut shin. I got those in a fight." By most accounts, this did not happen. When he was pulled from the water, he was naked and had only his father's watch. Many people suggested that he was able to survive because he was an outstanding athlete.

Jacques Futrelle had been reported as saved, but he had actually gone down with the ship. His daughter, Miss Virginia Futrelle, who was brought to New York from the Convent of Notre Dame in Baltimore, went to meet the *Carpathia*. Waiting with her was Mrs. Copeland of Boston, a sister of the writer. Both women were under the impression that Jacques Futrelle had been saved. When Mrs. Futrelle left the *Carpathia* alone, the two women wanted to know where her husband was. After composing herself, Mrs. Futrelle said he was coming on another ship. Then she told the truth. There was no other ship!

Once the ladies became composed after the truth was known, Mrs. Futrelle said her husband had died a hero after making sure she was safely in a lifeboat. She also commented that the only men who were saved were those who had "sneaked into the lifeboat or were picked up after the *Titanic* sunk." It is easy to understand why she would be so vehement in her condemnation of those men in lifeboats since her husband died a man and not a craven coward.

The Richmond newspapers were still reporting on the size of the *Titanic*. There was a picture of Main Street with the *Titanic* superimposed on it. The ship extended from the First National Bank building, past the Mutual Building, past the American National Bank Building and a little bit past the Travelers Building. This illustration provided a visual indication of the size of the lost ship.

In 1912, Richmonders frequently wrote poems about the loss of the *Titanic* and sent them to the newspapers to be published. This poem was written by a person who signed his name as "X."

> *O* Titanic*!* Titanic*! You symbol of strength.*
> *Against the natural forces your endurance had no length;*
> *You, ill-fated giant, were an atom on the sea,*
> *When a simple mass of congealed water bore down on thee.*

To capture the tone of the arrival of the *Carpathia*, this summary was published: "The silence of death prevailed being broken by the grief of some whose sobs found only sympathy in the hearts of those who remained uncomforted. The sorrowful silence was intensely oppressive and pervaded the souls of even those who welcomed the survivors of the *Titanic*." Indeed, the silence of death reached from the Old World to the New World.

The *Evening Journal* in an editorial observed that the *Titanic* story "is one of the most culpable seekings after financial glory at the expense of human risk and of transcendental heroism of men in the face of certain death that ever lined the annals of any page." The editorial lauded the conduct of Captain Smith and suggested that J. Bruce Ismay issued "criminal orders for utmost speed against all hazards under which this noble mariner was working and under which the *Titanic* was hurried to destruction; but in the vision of such sublime and transcended heroism, there is little thought aught else."

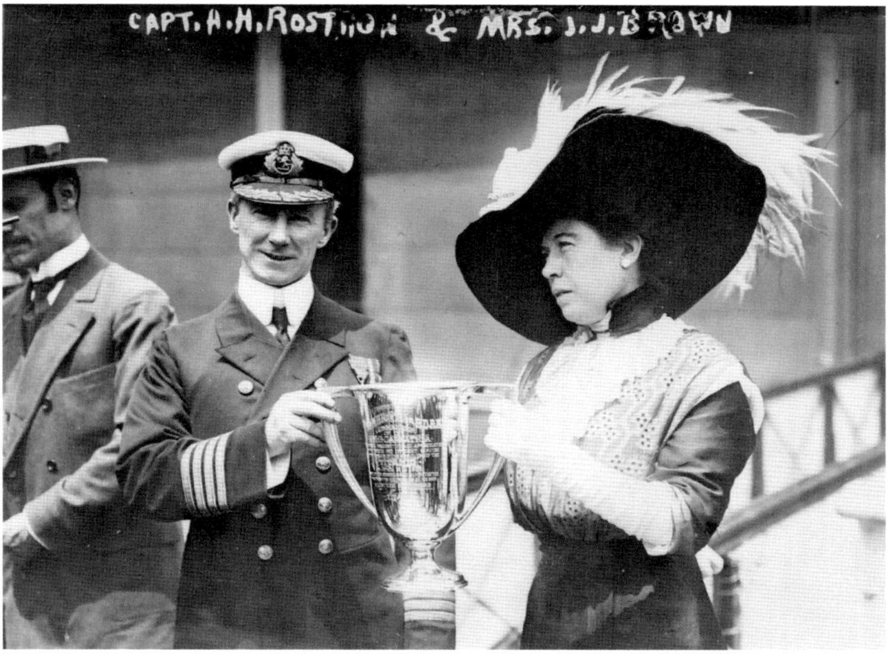

Captain Arthur Rostron was presented a trophy by the "Unsinkable" Molly Brown. *Courtesy of the Library of Congress.*

With the arrival of the *Carpathia*, many of the questions about the *Titanic*'s last night would be answered. In the days ahead, Richmonders would learn about the heroes and the cowards. Names like Ismay, Lightoller, Rostron, Daniel, Smith and many others would become household words.

Chapter 15

Saturday, April 20, 1912

There's no story told of true heroes bold,
That can dim the honor due.
To the martyrs brave,
In their nameless grave.
—Mark Beam

The news of the *Titanic* covered almost every page of the local newspapers this Saturday. Once the *Carpathia* docked, survivors began to be interviewed and their stories reported in the press. Additional news was coming from the Senate committee. Probably the most sensational story focused on J. Bruce Ismay.

The *Times Dispatch* reported in large type: "J. Bruce Ismay Tells [the Senate committee] in Whispers How He Escaped Death by Leaving the Sinking *Titanic* in Lifeboat with Women." This was made even more damning when the newspaper also carried on its front page this statement: "Quietly men wait for certain death as the ship goes down." It was obvious that J. Bruce Ismay did not wait for certain death. But the press was not finished with him.

It was revealed that he wanted the *Titanic*'s crew members who had survived to be returned to England as soon as possible. There were several positions taken on this information. Ismay contended that the crew should be reunited with their families as soon as possible, but it was also suggested that Ismay wanted them to get back to England and out of the jurisdiction of the United States before they could be questioned by the Senate committee.

It was reported that the White Star liner RMS *Cedric* was being held in New York to take Ismay and the crew members back to England. However, Mr. Ismay and the crew were kept in New York. There would be no escape from the Senate committee.

But this was only the beginning of the assault on Ismay. Even his appearance came under attack. It was reported, "Ismay talks with his head tilted back viewing his listener as from a great height. His attitude is that of a man who is used to looking down on his listeners." If this was not enough, it was pointed out that he was buying a new wardrobe to replace the one that was now at the bottom of the Atlantic. A reporter told his readers that Ismay backed away from him and looked at him with disdain.

A member of the Senate committee also joined in the attack. He asserted, "I do not believe that [Ismay] got into the last lifeboat, but if he did, it was cowardly to take any lifeboat for the managing director of this line who, with his Board of Directors, is criminally responsible for this appalling tragedy." It was also claimed that Ismay was responsible for the *Titanic* taking the northern route, which resulted in the collision with the iceberg. The final comment was "that he risked the life of his entire ship to make a speedy passage." This information was reportedly "dragged from his lips." The conclusion was that Ismay was responsible for the *Titanic*'s tragedy that "permitted 1,500 of her passengers and crew to be swallowed up by the sea." The headline for the article was as follows: "Ismay a Coward to Take Lifeboat." The newspaper then reported on other passengers.

Robert Daniel continued to be the focus of many stories. It was now reported that he left the *Carpathia* "half dead and incoherent." It was also reported again and again that Jacques Futrelle died like a hero. His widow continued to assert that "the only men saved were those who sneaked into lifeboats." Was she thinking of J. Bruce Ismay? Probably!

Many newspapers, including the *Times Dispatch*, reported that some "foreigners" did not act like heroes. For example, it was reported that "among those rescued from the sinking *Titanic* were six Chinese, who had stowed themselves away in one of the vessel's lifeboats before she left England. When the crash came on Sunday night, the Chinese did not become excited. They knew the lifeboats would be lowered if there was any danger of the Giant ship going down. All had shawls and when they heard the shouts of those on board that women were to be saved first, they covered themselves with their shawls, leading the crew to believe they were women. In the darkness they escaped detection. It was not known they were Chinese until they were taken on board the *Carpathia*. When it was discovered what they had done, some of the *Carpathia*'s crew wanted to toss them into the sea, but they were put in irons instead." There was a tendency to believe that all Anglo-Saxons acted properly. This was certainly not the case.

Richmonders continued to submit their poems about the *Titanic* to the Richmond newspapers, and a number of them were published. Although long forgotten, they captured the feelings of Richmonders during this tragic time. Many poems focused on the deaths of heroic men.

Titanic

Hail and farewell to those who with calm eye
Accepted death upon that fatal morn,
That shivering women and weak babies forlorn
Might through their sacrifice to safety fly
Farewell and hail! Brave and true gentlemen;
Sailor or landsman, steerage or millionaire,
Going to doom with hearts as debonair.
As if to strike warm hands with friends again;
O, God! That we the lesson might receive;
If man for man will gladly die at need.
Sure man for man may live, we must believe;
Not death, but life, is love's most blessed need.
Heroic deaths world-lost cannot retrieve;
Heroic lives alone must do the deed.
—FCW

The newspaper also published this poem:

And ye, great ice lumps, that with pounding thumps
And with a crunching noise, sound the loud buoys.
Thou, sobbing son, wandering over the lea.
Lend all thy moans to the funeral groans.
Thou, Mother Earth, hide in thy bosom the birth
Of tossing wrong that passed for Titan strong;
That played with the wild, mad waves and winds that wave;
And that grinding thing from the Arctic ring.
Unveil, and weep thou, fair maid of the mist,
For an ogre stole thy mantle and thole.
—E.F.S.

There were also many letters published that were written by Richmonders. Nellie Parker Henson wrote, "Reading the account of the terrible tragedy of the *Titanic*, I realized as never before that man is truly made in the image of God! Rich men dying that even peasant women and women's maids might live! It proves that in this age of selfishness 'woman' is still sacred to man." The writer continued, "I feel like mingling my tears with every mother who lost a son and every woman who lost a husband. That God will comfort and help the mothers and widows and orphans left so desolate by this disaster is the prayer of one who, too, had 'loved long since, and lost awhile.'"

On Saturday, the newspapers across America announced that Sunday services would honor the dead of the *Titanic*. As one writer put it, "Throughout the United States tomorrow morning and evening, special prayers for the souls of those who perished when the steamship *Titanic* sank will be offered."

Since it was a Saturday, many churches published their Sunday worship schedule, and a few churches published the sermon topic. The sermon topic at Grace Street Presbyterian was "The Law of the Sea." At Grace Street Baptist, the sermon topic was "Lessons from the Great Disaster," and at Centenary Methodist Church, the sermon was "The *Titanic* Disaster and Its Message to the Modern World." At Highland Park Methodist, the sermon topic was "Lessons from the Sinking of the *Titanic*." At Fairmount Baptist, the topic was "The *Titanic* Disaster." At St. John's German Evangelical Church, the sermon was "God's Providence and the *Titanic* Disaster." It was noted that the service was to be entirely in German. At Bainbridge Street Baptist, the sermon topic was "What Has God to Do with Accidents and Calamities."

On Friday night, the city's Jewish congregations held their services for those lost on the *Titanic*. A memorial service for the victims of the *Titanic* was conducted at the Jewish Sir Moses Montefore Congregation. This congregation also started a relief fund for those who had sailed on the fatal voyage of the *Titanic* and needed assistance.

Rabbi E.N. Calisch of Temple Beth Ahabah spoke to his congregation about the loss of the *Titanic* and posed this question: "Why were millions lavished upon appurtenances of luxury, beggarly hundreds denied for emergencies?" He suggested this question should be uppermost in the public mind and then concluded his sermon by asserting, "The world will be richer by this disaster—not richer in the commercial sense, but richer by reason of the fine examples of nobility and heroism offered by the men and women on board the sinking vessel." His congregation was profoundly moved by his sermon.

It was on this Saturday that the *Richmond Planet*, Richmond's African American newspaper, published an editorial on the *Titanic*. In the editorial entitled "Belshazzar's Feast," John Mitchell Jr., the iconic editor of the newspaper, wrote: "Some of the wealthiest people in the world secured reservations at exorbitant expense for the privilege of being passengers upon the maiden trip of this sea leviathan. Pleasure reigned supreme. Wine and liquor, games and other amusements were all in evidence, and the revelry which was taking place had never been equaled in the history of the world. Joy was unconfined and God was apparently forgotten." The writer continued his line of thought by writing: "The wealth of the American nation was represented. Petted children of fortune, careless of the way of the miser, now sweeping over the land, had spent millions for diamonds, jewelry and all the finery that the palatial cities of Europe afforded. They were coming home in triumph." Then the writer suggested that God had sent an iceberg that was "described as this hidden messenger of death that had stolen upon time in the midst of their fancied security and they had been weighed in the balances and found wanting. They went down to a watery grave, an unwilling sacrifice in the crowning blunder of the age." The writer concluded that the loss of the *Titanic* "was God's way; His will be done, not ours." By writing letters and poems, Richmonders were able to share their feelings and express their frustrations. This was an important outlet.

A man in New York apparently had no such outlet. He could not deal with the disaster and was convinced that the "wreck was the work of the Lord to punish the people for their sins." He became so violent that he was arrested and sent to a hospital for the insane. This story in the *New York Tribune* of April 20 was widely circulated.

Chapter 16

Sunday, April 21, 1912

You know it must have been awful
With those people on the sea
It's said that they were singing
Nearer, My God, to Thee
While some were homeward bound
Fifteen hundred had to drown
It was sad when that great ship went down.
—William and Versey Smith

This Sunday was the unofficial memorial day for the *Titanic*. The newspapers reported, "Richmond pastors will preach this morning and tonight on the great disaster of the steamer *Titanic*." The *Times Dispatch* stated, "While there will be no special memorial services conducted in Richmond, the lesson of the great tragedy will be impressed vigorously on the minds of the city congregations today." Most church leaders remembered the *Titanic* in their services and ended the service with the singing of "Nearer, My God, to Thee." The details of these services would appear in Monday's newspapers.

It had been a week since the *Titanic* had hit the iceberg, and the local newspapers still ran headlines about the tragedy. The front page this Sunday focused on the many iceberg warnings that the *Titanic* had received and ignored. Instead of responding to the warnings and slowing down, the *Titanic* continued "at its highest speed." Obviously, Richmonders and everybody else wanted to know why these warnings were not heeded.

People also wanted to know if First Officer Murdoch, who was in command when the *Titanic* struck the iceberg, had committed suicide. The press reported that Murdoch had refused to leave Captain Smith, who was standing on the bridge. As the two officers stood together, Murdoch shot himself in the head and fell into the water. The next day, this idea was rejected by his relatives who lived in Richmond.

An editorial praised the saving of women and children and attacked the behavior of some of the men who were trying to explain how they had survived while some of the women and children had died. The writer commented:

> *Some of them* [the men saved] *are trying to explain and shield the reactions of instincts that they find are rotten at the core. Of these is the pugnacious fool who in some way was saved among the women. When he reached New York, a reporter asked him the direct question of how he came to escape under such circumstances. The gentleman knocked him down. That is the complete definition of a coward. His instinct was so decayed in his heart that he sacrificed manhood for life. It is a good thing that the hearts of millionaires and peasants showed no yellow streaks, resulting either from luxury or poverty.*

Over and over again the message was that men were expected to sacrifice their lives to save the women and children, and those men who survived were expected to explain why they were still alive. This was not always easy to do!

Although the *Titanic* had been on the bottom of the Atlantic for less than a week, a play about it was already being produced in Richmond. The Lubin Theater advertised a slide show that would tell the story of the *Titanic*, including pictures of the iceberg that caused the accident. At the same theater, there was another show: Anton Zinka and His Musical Dogs.

Mrs. Henry Harris, whose husband went down with the *Titanic*, planned to produce a play about the tragedy. She wrote, "Fifteen hundred people were not drowned on the *Titanic;* 1,500 people were murdered, cruelly and foully murdered. That's the story, the true story, that I will tell the world as soon as I am able." At the same time, the mayor of Chicago forbade any types of plays or movies to be shown or performed in that city about the disaster.

In a report from London published by the *Times Dispatch*, it was revealed that fifty bellboys on the *Titanic* "went to their death smiling and joking, taking great delight in breaking the rules against smoking." A quartermaster on the ship wrote, "I saw them standing around various parts of the ship, smoking cigarettes and joking with the passengers. Not a single one of these boys tried to get into a lifeboat." None survived.

The news of the latest developments and revelations about the *Titanic* continued to be reported in headlines spread across the front pages of the morning and evening newspapers. It was a story that would not go away.

Chapter 17

Monday, April 22, 1912

Every lighthouse speaks eloquently of some shipwreck.
—The Reverend Dr. W.L. Young, Centenary Methodist Church

The headlines were focused on finding bodies floating in the Atlantic Ocean. Two wireless messages had been received from the cable steamer CS *Mackay-Bennett*, the ship sent by the White Star Line to retrieve bodies from the ocean. The ship was dispatched even before the *Carpathia* arrived in the Port of New York. Upon searching the site of the sinking, the *Mackay-Bennett* reported that sixty-four bodies had been recovered, including the body of John Jacob Astor. He was easy to identify by his gold watch, a diamond ring and a collar with the monogram JJA. He was tagged as body 124. The class system even prevailed in death. First-class passengers were placed in coffins and embalmed. The others were put in bags on ice. Over one hundred of the bodies recovered could not be identified. They were buried at sea in a mass funeral conducted by an Anglican clergyman from the Halifax Cathedral.

But the news in the Richmond newspapers continued to focus on two men who escaped from the *Titanic*: J. Bruce Ismay and Robert Daniel. In defending his actions, Ismay continued to assert that he had not been consulted by Captain Smith and that he had made no suggestions on how the ship should be navigated. He claimed to have been just an ordinary passenger on the ship and that he never suggested that the *Titanic* should try to set some sort of speed record. Although Ismay was desperately seeking to justify his behavior, the fact that he was alive while others were dead was enough to make people call him a coward and to treat him with disdain. Nothing he could say or do would change the minds of most of the people. His name was being changed in some circles to "J. Brute Ismay." One lady commented, "He has drunk the Babylonian cup to the dregs and God's rebuke is at hand."

Robert Daniel's story continued to be a front-page headline. The fact that he was pulled from the water by people in a lifeboat avoided the stigma attached to Ismay, who was in a lifeboat when it was lowered into the water. Daniel also reported that he had seen Ismay and said that he advised Ismay that he was being criticized by the other survivors. To add to the negative comments, Daniel reported that he had to sleep on the floor of the *Carpathia* while Ismay slept in a plush, locked stateroom.

The Monday newspaper gave a lot of space to the sermons preached on the subject of the *Titanic* on Sunday under the title "Moral Lesson in *Titanic* Tragedy." The general theme of these sermons was that those who went down with the *Titanic* did not die in vain. It was felt that as time passed, some good would emerge from the tremendous loss of life. It was hoped that the trinity of self-sacrifice, chivalry and valor would result in changes in ocean transportation with the use of more safety devices and lifeboats for every passenger. It was further believed that the "sinking proved that humans are frail and are utterly dependent on the living God." Most of Richmond's clergy did not seek to blame anyone for the disaster, but viewed it as the cost of "recklessness and greed traceable to modern conditions rather than to a particular person or persons." It was further contended that "progress always comes through tribulation and suffering," or to put it another way, "some must die in order that the race may live."

The sermon by the Reverend Dr. W.L. Young of Centenary Methodist Church was given extensive coverage in the newspaper. The minister contended that the calamity was avoidable; it did not have to happen. Although he did not place blame on anyone, he suggested that the loss of the *Titanic* is "in a sense a creature of conditions which today are leading us all to clamor for speed and which have back of them the mad rush to get rich." He then offered these words of comfort: "The hundreds whose bodies lie 2,000 fathoms below those icebergs have not died in vain. Moved by their death, the great nations will see to it that ships carry sufficient lifeboats, that they take routes beyond all possible contact with icebergs, and that the craving for speed and for luxury shall not interfere with safety." He also commented on the noble self-sacrifice of the men who died so women and children could live. Like many ministers, he reminded the congregation, "We are told that the band which, but, a short while before, had been playing the gayest of music, as the ship sank beneath the waves sounded out the hymns of faith 'Nearer, My God, to Thee' and 'Guide Me, O Thou Great Jehovah.'" He then closed with the thought that "eternity will furnish every opportunity to get things right."

Another sermon that was given extensive coverage in the *Richmond News Leader* was delivered by the Reverend G.T. Forester of Decatur Street Methodist Church. He preached on the topic "Save Our Souls." He reminded his congregation, "Man's power is nothing when opposed to the will of God." He made the point that the *Titanic* had everything it needed, but "on this occasion the power and knowledge of man was opposed to the will of God; the ship went down, taking with it 1,500 souls." For some reason, he felt one of the benefits of the sinking was "the closing of a number of theatres in New York City due to small attendance." In concluding his sermon, Reverend Forester observed, "Every passenger on the lost ship had made plans for their future after the arrival in New York. Millionaires, steerage passengers, and crew all had decided what course they would pursue after the docking of the *Titanic*. It was improbable, however, if any had left Southampton prepared to die, or with any plans made for such an event."

In New York City, a sermon preached by the Reverend Dr. Charles Parkhurst gained a great deal of attention across the nation. Dr. Parkhurst said, "The picture which presents itself before my eyes is that of the glassy, glaring eyes of the victims, staring meaninglessly at the gilded furnishing of this sunken palace of the sea; dead helplessness wrapped in priceless luxury; jewels valued in seven figures becoming the strange playthings of the queer creatures that sport in the dark depths. Everything for existence, nothing for life. Grand men, charming women, beautiful babies, all becoming horrible in the midst of the glittering splendor of a $10,000,000 casket!" A different tone was set by the Reverend Dr. Ernest Stires in a sermon preached at St. Thomas' Church in New York. Dr. Stires told his congregation, "The disaster has made of the whole human race a sorrowing family. The band played 'Nearer, My God to Thee' on its knees, sinking down into the depths. Today I hear from them from the heights, for they died a death worth dying, to teach us how to live a life worth living." A Baptist writer selected a different theme. He wrote as follows: "The wireless call for help has come from hundreds of millions of men and women going down in the night from the sinking craft of false religion and no religion to the bottomless abyss of despair."

In a book edited by Martin Breese and published right after the sinking, the editor wrote, "Angry is the word—for in all her triumph of perfection the *Titanic* was but man's latest insolence to the sea. Every article in her was a sheer defiance to the Deep's might and majesty. The ship is not the ocean's bride; steel hull and mast, whirling shaft and throbbing engine-heart (products, all, of serviceable wonderworking fire)—what kinship have these with the wild and watery waste? They are an affront and not an affinity for the cold and alien and elusive element that at all times threatens to overwhelm them." Many other books would carry this same theme.

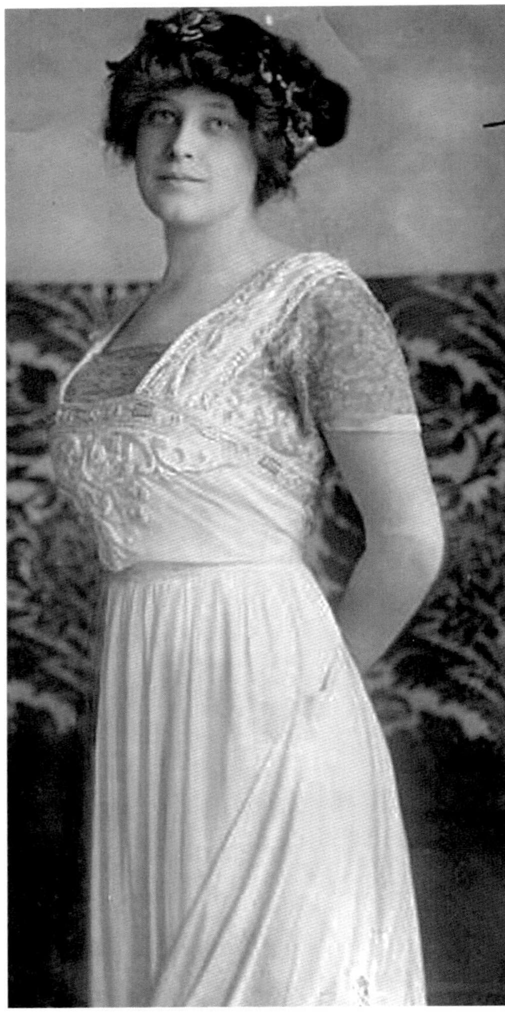

Madeleine Astor, wife of John Jacob Astor. *Courtesy of the Library of Congress.*

Although John Jacob Astor had died on the *Titanic* and his body had been pulled from the Atlantic and identified, he was not spared a measure of censure. It was reported that in 1910 he had divorced his wife and was forbidden to remarry in New York State. In August 1911, it was announced that he was engaged to be married to Miss Madeleine Force, who was eighteen years old while Mr. Astor was forty-seven. But Mr. Astor had a problem. Episcopal priests across the nation announced that they would refuse to marry the couple. He offered $1,000 to both a Baptist and a Methodist minister if they would perform the ceremony, but both refused. Eventually, they were married in the United States and then went to Egypt and Europe to wait for the gossip to die down.

While abroad, Mrs. Astor became pregnant, and the couple headed back to the United States on the *Titanic* to make sure the child was born in the United States. Reportedly, Mr. Astor was the richest man to be lost on the *Titanic*. But he was not a coward. He did what men were expected to do; he went down with the ship.

Letters and suggestions continued to be published. In the newspaper, one man proposed the following: "Could not the law require certain convoys to accompany these precious monsters, with fog horns, searchlights and tons of dynamite to shatter and scatter these ice mountains that menace human life?" And there was a very morbid letter by a professor at Johns Hopkins University explaining how the bodies of those lost on the *Titanic* would sink to the bottom of the sea. There was another suggestion that the bodies would sink and then suddenly pop to the surface. A reader of this debate would certainly be repulsed and wonder why it was even printed.

In the editorial section, a lengthy poem was published. It was written by a man from Charlottesville. The poem is as follows:

Tremble and be still! For the Lord hath spoken only;
And shall a man boast of his littleness
And trust in his human invention.
The sea hath swallowed them up, and their pride is sunk.
Behold the works of man! They shall perish;
His cunning machines shall break—
His engines shall obey the Law.
But the hand that made the engines is perverted!
The Man hath forgotten the law
The blind lead the blind, in their vanity,
And weakness is an aspiring virtue
So the mighty come to destruction
Eating and drinking they said, we are perfect;
We are become even as God.
In their steel ship they trusted.
Their gold glittered to blindness,
And they forgot the Law
In their strong tinseled palace they lusted.
They lived in idleness
And their luxury drowned them—
The sea closed over them
For they remembered not the Law!

The oxygen shall cut the ship,
And every man shall tremble;
The rust shall take her elements,
They all may learn the Law:
And this tale shall be told to the glory of the ever-living God.

Although the newspapers were filled with *Titanic* stories, there was still room for other news and advertisements. One story reported that King George and Queen Mary of England had asked that the cruel sport of pigeon shooting be stopped. It was revealed that the king and queen were pigeon fanciers, and the pigeon houses at Sandingham Palace were among the finest in the world. It was even suggested that the royal family spent as much on their pigeons as they did on their horses. Another story from England reported that a British inquiry was going to examine the *Titanic* tragedy. In the months ahead, the investigation would yield additional information about the tragic loss of the *Titanic*. This investigation would be to England what the United States Senate Investigation would be to the United States.

And there was an advertisement from Schwarzschild Brothers Jewelers that this was the "season of the engagement ring." Amid the sadness, life did continue on in Richmond, but the main topic of conversation remained the loss of the *Titanic*. The tragedy was so overwhelming and incomprehensible that it would remain a topic of conversation for generations.

Chapter 18

Tuesday, April 23, 1912

The Californian *not a dozen miles away*
Never heard the SOS 'cus the crew had hit the hay
Captain and crew never knew that ship was through
It was sad when that great ship went down.
—Unknown

Richmonders were shocked when they read this headline: "Frantic Appeals of Stricken Ship Are Not Answered." What was this about? It was revealed that a nearby ship did not respond and try to save those in "peril on the sea." This new revelation was disclosed at the United States Senate hearings when Fourth Officer Joseph Boxhall stated that a ship was in sight of the sinking *Titanic* but did not respond. He testified, "The ship could not have been more than five miles away and was steaming toward the *Titanic*. So close was it that I could plainly see its masthead lights and the red side light." He also said that he tried to get the ship to respond by firing rockets, flashing a light to signal in Morse code and using the wireless, with no results. He further testified that Captain Smith and others believed the ship had seen the *Titanic* and was going to respond. Richmonders, as well as the nation, were appalled at the news. People rightfully had difficulty understanding why a ship so close to the *Titanic* did not respond to help. It was believed that this callous indifference cost many lives. This would open an entirely new line of questioning and introduce a new culprit into the mix: Captain Stanley Lord was the commanding officer of the Leland Line ship

SS *Californian*, which was the ship identified as the one that would not come to help.

On a more positive note, it was also reported that the Richmond Blues would honor Major Archibald Butt. The order was as follows:

> *In honor of a brave man and a gallant soldier, who sacrificed his life in the cause of humanity and whose death has cast a shadow of sorrow over the soldiery of this great nation be they regulars or volunteers, the officers of this battalion are ordered to wear the usual sign of mourning as a mark of respect to the memory of Major Archibald W. Butt, United States Army.*
>
> *E. W Bowles*
> *Commanding Officer*

A more lasting tribute to the *Titanic* was proposed by James Rodgers of Ashland, Virginia. He wrote, "The question arises, would not we as a fitting completion to the sacrifices of the men in their obedience to that law of the sea and to the love and devotion of those who went down to their death, refusing life rather than life without loved ones, and to the band who comforted the dying with a thought of the life to come, should not we erect some reminder of these acts of heroism and of the heritage which is entrusted to the care of the generations to follow us after our death?" In the years ahead, there would be many monuments erected in honor of those who died in the waters of the cold Atlantic Ocean.

Even though the *Titanic* tragedy had happened less than two weeks ago, there was an advertisement in the newspaper as follows: "Agents, Oceans greatest tragedy. Gigantic steamship *Titanic* goes to the bottom on her maiden trip. Multimillionaires, authors, statesmen, and immigrants share the same watery grave. Our great book, profusely illustrated, will tell the thrilling story with personal accounts of heroic self-sacrifice, marvelous escapades, and terrible sufferings. Be first in the field and reap a golden harvest. Liberal commission. Prospectus now ready. Sales outfit free. Send 10 cents to cover the cost of mailing. The Thompson Pub. Co., St Louis, Mo." It is amazing that in 1912, a book could be published so soon after the disaster, and it seems somewhat insensitive for the suggestion to be made that a bookseller could make a lot of money while families still grieved for loved ones at the bottom of the ocean. Many more books would be published in the next few weeks, including the one purchased by my great-grandmother. While not always accurate, they did mold the opinions of the readers—opinions that are still part of the fabric of the *Titanic* story.

Chapter 19

Wednesday, April 24, 1912

The ship that rode on noonday tide
Rode forth to open sea,
But gone are the gladness, and hope, and pride
For the Northern Ocean's depths could hide
A mightier power than she.
—Father Frank Browne, SJ

Over a week had passed since the *Titanic* had sunk, and Richmonders were still seeing its story on the front pages of the newspaper. A lead story in the *Times Dispatch* speculated that "a few dollars might have saved the vessel and human freight." The few dollars could have provided binoculars or telescopes for the lookouts that might have enabled them to see the iceberg in time for the *Titanic* to avoid hitting it.

But a more important story focused on the *Californian* and why she did not come to the aid of the stricken *Titanic*. Captain Lord denied the allegation by stating that his ship, the *Californian*, was seventeen to nineteen miles away. He discredited the members of the crew who claimed that the *Californian* was much closer by observing, "Sailors will tell almost anything when they are ashore." This rebuttal would soon be challenged, and Captain Lord would become the personification of a man who simply let people die.

Richmonders continued to turn to their faith as a way to deal with the loss. At the Cathedral of the Sacred Heart, a solemn requiem Mass was celebrated for the repose of the souls of those who perished in the sinking of the *Titanic*. Bishop Dennis O'Connell told the faithful, "We are assembled in this church, not to censure, but to pray. It is a holy and wholesome thought to pray for the dead that they may be loosed from their sins. God is a God of the living and not of the dead. For to him, there are no dead and we all live unto Him. We are here to pray for comfort for those that survived the disaster." He then spoke directly to the loss of the *Titanic* by saying, "In my opinion society is on a higher plane today than it was a fortnight ago. In the future, women and children first will be a law and not a mere sentiment of humanity. Too long have the weak been crushed and ground under the feet of the heartless strong. Respect for the weak was promulgated anew from the decks of the sinking vessel." He concluded by stating, "Two lessons I find—one for the individual and one for society. For the individual, a fuller recognition of the sovereignty of God. No unsinkable ship nor Tower of Babel can ever overthrow his supremacy. For society, a life lived nearer to God, nearer to what is noble and high, ready to answer no matter how suddenly we are called. For society, respect for the weak, suppression of brute force under the supremacy of God. Never to trample a woman or child, not only in a wreck at sea, nor even during the stress of life ashore. That is civilization; that is religion. And if we heed the lesson, the disaster of the *Titanic* is a boon for humanity—salvation through a cross." Bishop O'Connell was one of many clergymen who would seek to find some good in the disaster. And people certainly needed to find something positive in the tragic loss of life.

The newspaper reported that a service would be held at St. Paul's Episcopal Church the next day, which was St. Mark's Day. Reportedly, this service was in response to many requests from the Richmond community.

There were so many letters and poems being sent to the newspapers across the nation that some editors would only publish works by established writers and poets. This was not the case in Richmond. Richmonders continued to write, and the *Times Dispatch* and the other newspapers continued to publish poems about the *Titanic*. This lengthy poem was written by a Richmonder.

Down in the bowels of the deep blue sea;
Rests the Titanic, *a giant was she*
Though built to ply from shore to shore,
She touched but one and will touch no more.

On that dark and dismal night,
When captain and crew thought all was right

Somewhere hidden in the path she chose
A giant iceberg suddenly arose.

And before the crew had time to act
The gallant show on the iceberg crashed
Terrible must have been the scene,
They heard the women and children scream.

To hear the agonizing groans
Of women and children so far from home.
Little expecting when they went to sleep
To find a grave in the briny deep.

But God, the ruler of the sea and sky.
Bids us ever to be ready to die,
He says death comes as a thief in the night
And what he says is always right.

Of passengers and crew but few were saved—
Hundreds found a watery grave.
So long as hills the ocean ride
So long as stars shine in the skies
Catastrophe such as silence will be
And when no catastrophe and then no sea.
—J.M. Norman, Barton Heights

While there were still many letters and poems being published about the men and the loss of the *Titanic*, the newspapers also published some short pithy comments, such as the following: "Why all this grilling to make Mr. Ismay explain [his survival] when it is as clear as daylight that he just got into that [life]boat to assure enough ballast." Andrew Carnegie, the steel magnate, commented, "What was the *Titanic* doing up among the ice when she had the whole Atlantic Ocean open and free?" And the final observation: "The more haste, the less speed."

Chapter 20

Thursday, April 25, 1912

Earth to Earth, Dust to Dust, Ashes to Ashes.
—Book of Common Prayer

And the sea gave up its dead.
—Revelations 20:13

Richmonders who paid two cents for their morning newspaper opened it to see this story on page one: "Bodies Strewn among Atlantic Waves." And the story continued on to report that corpses were continuing to drift many miles from the grave of the *Titanic* and were being picked up by the cable ship *McKay-Bennet*. One can only imagine what it must have been like to pull dead bodies out of the ocean, try to identify them and then place them in coffins or on ice. Surely, it took an emotional toll on the men as their ship floated among the dead.

When the *McKay-Bennet* was filled to capacity with bodies, the cable ship CS *Minia* was dispatched to relieve her. Unlike the *McKay-Bennet*, there was no clergy aboard to commit the dead to the ocean, only the crew and undertakers. The ship's cargo included one hundred coffins, one hundred tons of ice and a quantity of iron to be used as weights to sink the unidentified dead to the bottom of the ocean.

There was another story similar to the story about the inaction of the *Californian*. When the SS *Mount Temple* docked at St. Johns, New Brunswick, "A passenger claimed to have seen the *Titanic* sink and the ship did not respond."

The captain of the *Mount Temple* had to defend himself. He stated that he had received a "CQD message at 12:30 a.m. and immediately responded to the site of the sinking." He testified that he had "stayed at the scene of the sinking until he was advised by the captain of the *Carpathia* that there was nothing more he could do." Although some passengers alleged that he was only five miles from the sinking *Titanic*, the captain of the *Mount Temple* was able to show that he was fifty miles away. Apparently tension between the captain and some passengers and crew members resulted in this unjustified claim. The captain was exonerated, and his accusers were never identified.

Against these stories of finding bodies and telling lies, there was a story about the community service of remembrance held at St. Paul's Episcopal Church on St. Mark's Day. This was a special service "as a memorial to the men who heroically sacrificed their lives for others in the sinking of the *Titanic*." The service included a communion service. After remarking on the brave men who died so others might live, the rector made this observation: "Their glory and heroism caused the beauty of their sacrifice to tower above the shattered wreckage. Life is not measured by its length, but by its quality." For the faithful, this service brought a measure of comfort.

The newspaper used several pages to report some of the testimony given at the Senate committee meeting, which was now being held in Washington, D.C. Frederick Fleet, who was the lookout who first reported the iceberg, was asked these questions:

> *"When you were on the* Titanic, *were your eyes examined?"*
> *"Yes."*
> *"How often."*
> *"Frequently."*
> *"Can you distinguish colors?"*
> *"Yes, sir."*

Robert Hichens was at the wheel when the *Titanic* hit the iceberg. He offered the following testimony: "The officers had been warned to look out for small ice. The first I knew of the collision was when the order came down from the bridge, 'Berg Ahead.'" He continued: "The first officer rushed over to give the order 'Hard a starboard,' and Hichens responded, 'Helm hard over, sir,' but by that time we were into the berg. We could hear the grinding on it. I stayed at the wheel until 12:23 a.m."

Fifth Officer Harold Lowe was questioned by Senator Smith. Smith asked, "Do you know what an iceberg is composed of?"

Harold Lowe responded, "Ice, I suppose, sir." This question was frequently cited by the British as an example of lack of knowledge by the Senate committee.

Many poems and letters were still being published in the newspapers about that fateful night. Benjamin C. Moomaw wrote a poem that includes these verses:

The fateful hour, the surge of power,
The silence of the sea;
The Death that swiftly rode that night
On wings of majesty.
The life that soon gave back its vision to the skies
The shadowy harrow of the deep and all its mysteries.

And leave as but a lesser thing the life that's only given,
That we may win the wider worlds when all these bonds are riven.
And find amid the glories which no eloquence can tell
How 'tis a prophet voice that speaks the tardiest FAREWELL.

For over a week, the story of the *Titanic* was front-page news. Some stories were repeated or amplified, and some new stories were added as more information became available through the Senate committee. The loss of so many lives cast a pall of sadness over Richmond and the nation.

Chapter 21

FRIDAY, APRIL 26, 1912

There the brave men stood,
Like true heroes should
With their hearts in faith sublime.
And their names shall be fond memory
Until the end of Time.
And the band was bravely playing
The song of cross and crown
"Nearer, My God, to Thee"
As the ship went down.
—Mark Beam and Harold Jones

Today, there was a front-page story that the *Olympic*, the sister ship of the *Titanic*, was back in service following a strike by the ship's firemen over the safety of the ship's lifeboats. The ship was stopped off the coast of the Isle of Wight while the strike was being settled. The *Olympic* resumed its trip when the firemen were convinced the lifeboats were seaworthy. It was reported that the passengers on the *Olympic* entertained themselves by flying kites off the stern of the ship during the negotiations.

There were stories about the burials of those who had been brought to Halifax, Nova Scotia, by the "ships of death" that had been dispatched by the White Star Line to collect the bodies of the dead. At the many funerals in Halifax, this verse from Psalm 90 was frequently used: "The days of our years are three score and ten; and if by reason of strength they be four score

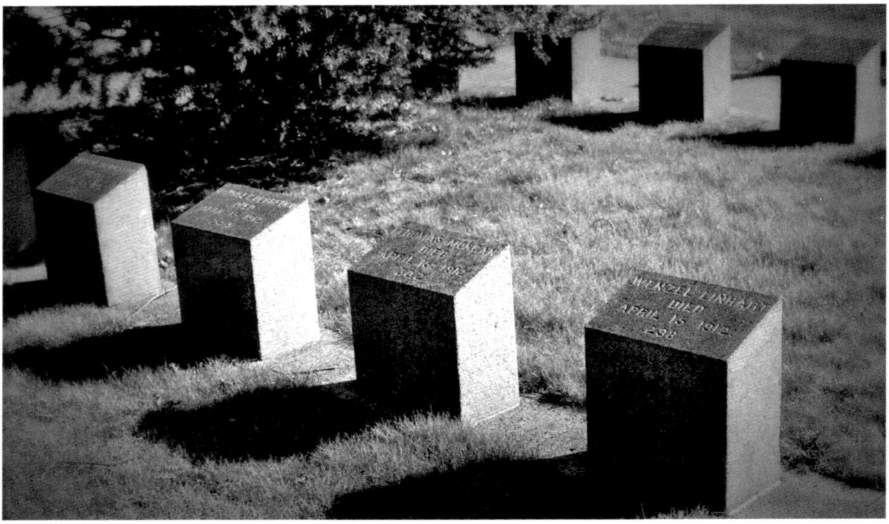

Titanic section of Fairview Cemetery in Halifax, Nova Scotia, where over one hundred of those who died on the ship are buried. *Courtesy of Wikimedia Commons.*

years, yet is their strength labour and sorrows, for it is soon cut off and we fly away."

Concerned about his chief military aide, Major Archibald Butt, President William Howard Taft sent the USS *Chester* to see what could be found out about him. Having no success, the president sent a military officer to Halifax, Nova Scotia, to see if he could identify the remains of Major Butt. His remains were never found.

Another man who died in the tragedy was Charles M. Hays, the president of the Grand Trunk Railroad. In his memory, all Grand Trunk trains were stopped for five minutes; all office work was stopped for the same amount of time. This story was followed by a reminder of the dangers of icebergs. The North German Lloyd steamer *Rhein* docked in Baltimore. The captain reported seeing twenty icebergs and a number of floating bodies and wreckage.

There was an interesting letter in the newspaper stating that safety at sea would improve following the loss of the *Titanic*. However, the writer then made the transition to comparing the *Titanic* to a mystical ship named the *Tuberculosis*. The ship *Tuberculosis* claimed five thousand people each year in Virginia. The writer made the rather graphic comment, "No barking like that of dogs will echo from souls face to face with death, but the stifled groans and whispered farewells will pierce loving hearts for days and months." The comments ended with the thought: "The lessons of the *Titanic* are manifold. But there is none for [the ship *Tuberculosis*]." Obviously, the writer thought something needed to be done to help those with this lung disease.

And for those who read the advertisements at the end of the newspaper, they would find three books about the *Titanic* for sale. One of the books being advertised was the *Sinking of the* Titanic, by Jay Mowbray, which is the book my great-grandmother purchased. My great-grandmother would have read these words from the book: "But now as a bolt from the blue, and as a forecast of the final mortal terrors of the Day of Judgment, comes the message that of 2,300 souls aboard but 700—chiefly women and children—have been saved." The author then made this observation: "The sole redeeming circumstance is that heroes met their deaths like men, and that human love was victorious over human terror and mightier than Death and the open grave of the remorseless deep."

Until World War I, there were many books published about the *Titanic*, and these books kept the story alive when it had faded from the headlines.

Chapter 22

Saturday, April 27, 1912

Lost on the great Titanic
Sinking to rise no more,
The number, sixteen hundred
That failed to reach the shore.
—Unknown

On this Saturday, the news of the *Titanic* was sparse. The primary focus was again on the growing controversy that the *Californian* saw the distress rockets being fired from the *Titanic* but ignored them. A crew member on the *Californian* claimed that lives could have been saved if the ship had responded. Other crewmen testified that Captain Lord saw these rockets but made no effort to get up steam and go to the rescue. Captain Lord vigorously denied the accusations. To further support his claim of innocence, the captain reported that the wireless operator was off duty and did not receive any distress calls from the *Titanic.* Still, a big question had been raised, and Captain Lord was put in a very unfortunate light in which he remains to this day.

The newspaper continued to publish poems by local residents. One poem had these lines:

Pray to the God above them,
In truth to save their souls;
For them a last sad requiem.
The awful ocean rolls.

She sinks—her wealth, her power;
No more the world's proud queen.

No vestige of her glory
Above the sea is seen.

Ah! What can be the answer
From out her ocean bed?
Canst tell the whole disaster
"Till the sea gives up its dead"

Her loss in millions may be told.
Her glory be forgot;
But in God's great forever
Those souls will perish not.
—F.C.M. Chase City

And there was something new on the editorial pages. Just as one writer wrote about the *Titanic* and the ship *Tuberculosis*, another contributor asserted in a letter that if her candidate, Champ Clark, did not win the Democratic Party's nomination for president of the United States, the following might happen: "The life of this republic as our forefathers established it is at stake. The old landmarks of a free republic, free from the machinations of the classes, free from the shameful bossism of plutocracy, free from the oppression of the plain people by a damnable taxation system are in danger of being stricken down and lost forever. If the corrupt and corrupting wing of the Republican Party should defeat us in November, I fear the republic, like the *Titanic* off Newfoundland Banks, will go down to be seen no more forever." Within two weeks of the tragedy, the *Titanic* was being used as a synonym for disaster.

Another writer was concerned that Congress was spending so much time with its investigations that it was not spending enough time in support of the United States Army in the border conflict with Mexico led by Pancho Villa. The writer then commented that soldiers along the border need the same attention as the "dead in the quiet depths of the Atlantic."

For almost two weeks, Richmonders had been reading about the *Titanic* tragedy. They had read and reread the stories of how one iceberg could turn joy to sorrow, life to death, hope to despair, unsinkable to sinkable and "Alexander's Rag Time Band" to "Nearer, My God, to Thee." Some people blamed the disaster on a vengeful God, some on an arrogant man, some on an incompetent captain and others on the need for God to destroy those whose wealth clouded their vision of the poor. In the final analysis, Richmonders came to their own conclusions about why and how it happened. As a city with many houses of worship, many Richmonders believed that SOS was not a call for help from a ship in distress but a plea that God would "Save Our Souls."

Chapter 23

Sunday, April 28, 1912

The ship was taking water
In the North Atlantic fog
When the first mate wrote
The last word in the log
The Captain tried to wire
But the wires were all on fire
Oh, it was sad when that great ship went down.
—Unknown

Two weeks after the *Titanic* hit the iceberg, the *Times Dispatch* published a special section on the disaster. The editor stated, "Now that the first shock of the *Titanic* disaster with the succession of wild rumors which it brought has given place to something like certain knowledge of what occurred on the terrible night that the giant liner plunged to the bottom of the sea, a complete narrative of the wreck is published at the request of many readers."

The front page continued the *Californian* controversy with the headline "Nation Aghast at Revelations about *Titanic*." The article suggested that all on board the *Titanic* might have been saved if the wireless operator on the *Californian* had been on duty or the distress rocket signals had been answered. Unfortunately, the law did not require wireless operators to be on duty for twenty-four hours. But people still could not understand why the *Californian* ignored the distress rockets fired in desperation from the *Titanic* and doomed the passengers.

Although the special section did not give Richmonders much new news, it did correct some earlier errors in reporting and provided a comprehensive review of the loss of the *Titanic*, as well as some intriguing sidelights, including a premonition of death.

It seems that the wife of the United States ambassador residing in Rome was an old friend of Major Archibald Butt. Apparently Major Butt had a severe emotional condition that his stay in Rome had done much to alleviate. In fact, he wanted to stay longer but had other commitments. The major confided to a friend that what he dreaded was a lingering death. He said that "he hoped that when the time came for him to die, he could be snuffed out like a candle and spared the lingering torture that is generally expected." For several hours, the major wondered if he should buy a ticket for the *Titanic*, but something seemed to be holding him back. But he eventually bought it, and his life was snuffed out as he wished it to be. Since the major had many friends in Richmond, the story was of great local interest.

Frances Courtney Baylor wrote a column for the special section of the newspaper entitled "The *Titanic* Tragedy." She commented that the *Titanic* was on everybody's mind. She contended that "nobody felt the least anxiety or mistrust about the *Titanic* before the accident. Nobody, after it happened, seems to have believed that she could possibly be lost under any conceivable circumstances." Baylor made the point that because of its size, people had different perspectives on what happened. She observed, "In Richmond, the man on one block would not see what the man on the next block saw at all." She had a lengthy list of condemnations, including the speed of the *Titanic* under the circumstances and the lack of provisions in the lifeboats. She suggested that most passengers prior to the accident had no more interest in lifeboats "than the passage of an ice wagon in January." She also pointed out the difficulties of launching lifeboats from a sinking ship and suggested that some other means needed to be developed.

Baylor quoted a railroad engineer, who pointed out, "Ships ought to be run more as trains are run." She then wrote that the engineer had said, "It is idiotic to engage about 100 musicians, waiters, cooks, stewards, bootblacks, and stewardesses for a boat, and only a handful of sailors to handle a huge, unwieldy, enormously costly ship to a piece of good luck to take such a ship from port to port over summer seas quite safely." She wrote that unlike the White Star Line, the Cunard Line "has well-disciplined seamen, looks carefully to the safety of its passengers, has never lost a ship, runs prudently at night, sounding constantly, and taking the temperature when likely to encounter ice, all the ordinary precautions under ordinary circumstances and extraordinary ones, when perils are to be encountered." She asserted, "All ships should have their wireless operators on duty for 24 hours to make sure distress calls are heard." She concluded by stating, "Who of us does not heartily thank God for wireless telegraphy—a thing unheard of even five years ago?"

In the special section, there were stories with the following titles: "Queen of the Sea's Awful Fate on Her First Trip Out"; "Heroism and Suffering as the Giant Liner Sinks"; "How the Wireless Cry CQD Brought Quick Aid"; "Four Days of Terrible Suspense Breeds Wild Rumors"; "*Carpathia* Brings the Rescued Survivors Ashore"; and "Unrivaled Size and Splendor of the Ill-Fated Ship." Basically, they were refined and expanded versions of stories previously published.

In a lengthy story on the ship's splendor, a reporter quoted these lines from a White Star Line brochure describing the *Titanic:* "Upon a dark, richly carpeted cloth which will further emphasize the delicacy and refinement of the paneling and act as a foil for the light dresses of the ladies, this company will assemble the apotheosis, surely, of ocean-going luxury and comfort. What more appropriate setting than this dignified Jacobean room redolent of the time when the Pilgrim Fathers set forth from Plymouth in their rude bark to brave the perils of the deep?" It was pointed out that the *Mayflower* and its Pilgrim passengers made it safely although their ship was only a little larger than one of the *Titanic*'s lifeboats.

The story of the *Titanic* was even known by children in Richmond. On the *Times Dispatch*'s children's page, a child had drawn, and the newspaper had printed, a picture of the ship along with pictures of birds and people. The child's picture showed the *Titanic* speeding across the ocean, but surely the young person knew its ultimate fate.

Chapter 24
Monday, April 29, 1912

Oh! Titanic, *monster of the sea*
All is rest and peace with thee.
The sun may shine, the rain may rain,
But on your decks never again.
—Chrystal Mohr

The *Titanic* story that interested Richmonders most on this day was that Robert Daniel of Philadelphia was in town to visit his mother, Mrs. J.R.V. Daniel. It was reported: "During the day many of Mr. Daniel's friends called to see him, and to all he gave a graphic description of the disaster." Apparently, he had recovered from the shock and suffering that he endured before being rescued by the *Carpathia.*

The news of the *Titanic* was again focused on the collecting of the bodies. It was reported that Atlantic storms prevented further search for the dead. It was also noted that the second vessel dispatched to collect the dead, the *Minia,* was returning to Halifax with only a few bodies on board. The captain of the ship reported that he did not have the bodies of any prominent persons on board. He indicated that he did not believe that the bodies of Major Archibald Butt and Mrs. Isidor Straus would ever be found. The ship did send the names of those recovered to the White Star Line. It also sent a wireless as follows: "Northerly gale, rough sea, and fog; nothing done; bodies much scattered; no groups; necessary steam over wide area; all vessels report no wreckage or bodies seen. Continuing search when weather modifies." In the same article it was reported that John Jacob Astor's family had arrived in Halifax in a private railroad car to take his body back to New York for burial.

There were many heroes on the *Titanic*, and in a letter to the editor, it was suggested that we need heroes in Richmond. The writer commented, "We have been talking a great deal of late of the heroism of the *Titanic* victims who refused to leave the ship in order that the women and children might be saved. But there is another kind of heroism—the heroism of daily life—the heroism of the lighter curse—the heroism of the sacrificed ambition—the heroism which for the sake of others' welfare takes up and bears the burden that no one else will lift. Who will fill the breach in Richmond?"

While Richmond was looking for heroes, the King of England sent this message to President Taft: "The Queen and I are anxious to assure you and the American nation of the great sorrow which we experienced of the terrible loss of life that has occurred among the American citizens, as well as among my own subjects, by the foundering of the *Titanic*. Our two countries are so intimately allied by ties of friendship and brotherhood that any misfortunes which affect the one must necessarily affect the other, and on the present terrible occasion they are both equal sufferers."

President Taft responded, "In the presence of the appalling disaster to the *Titanic*, the people of the two countries are brought into a community of grief through their common bereavement. The American people share in the sorrow of their kinsmen beyond the sea."

A common grief tightened the bonds of friendship between the two great nations. Frequently, a poem by Alfred Lord Tennyson was repeated when thoughts turned to the loss of the *Titanic*.

Sunset and evening star,
And one clear call for me.
And may there be no moaning of the bar,
When I put out to sea.

But such a tide as moving seems asleep,
Too full for sound and foam,
When that which drew from out the boundless deep
Turns again home.

Twilight and evening bell,
And after that the dark!

And may there be no sadness of farewell,
When I embark.

For tho' from out our Bourne of Time and Place
The flood may bear me far,
I hope to see my Pilot face to face
When I have crossed the bar.

After almost two weeks, Richmonders began to focus on other issues. There was a story about an irate rooster attacking a little girl. And a father wrote to the newspaper stating that his children were not being taught to spell in school. He claimed that on a geography test, his son misspelled the name of every country. When confronted, the teacher responded, "Spelling is not part of geography." The irate father immediately sent his children to a different school and boasted about his own ability as a speller because of his superior education. Richmond seemed to be getting back to normal.

Chapter 25

Tuesday, April 30, 1912

It was midnight on the sea,
Band playin' "Nearer, My God, to Thee"
Cryin', Fare thee, Titanic, *fare thee well.*
—Huddie Ledbetter

The big news was again about the Allen gang and the shootout at a Virginia courthouse. This story had been relegated to the back pages of the newspaper following the sinking of the *Titanic*. With over two weeks of *Titanic* news, the shootout returned to the front page.

There was still some more news about the *Titanic*. It was reported that the Senate committee was in the last stages of its inquiry, and it was believed that the officers and crew of the *Titanic* would soon be able to return home. However, there was a story from the British Foreign Affairs Office warning the House of Commons not to accept the findings of the Senate committee as "Gospel." In fact, it was suggested that no references be made to the Senate Report in Great Britain.

There was also a letter to the *Times Dispatch* criticizing the Senate committee. A writer asked, "Can it be possible that the investigation by the Senate of the *Titanic* disaster has any other meaning or motive than the desire to get at the causes of the catastrophe? Are the hearings by the specular court without political significance? We wonder." The writer suggested that the people's business was being delayed by the lengthy sessions concerning the loss of the *Titanic*. To make his point, the person wrote, "It may seem, in more ways than one, providential to these sedate gentlemen who, safely screened behind a thrilling tragedy, can eat of the lotus of innocent desuetude without running any risk of influencing popular feelings by action."

The newspaper continued to focus on the wealthy. It was reported that John Jacob Astor, in his will, provided for both his first and second wives. However, Astor did state in his will that if his second wife should remarry, she would no longer benefit from his estate. Many people thought this provision was mean-spirited. The bulk of his estate went to his son Vincent in the amount of $150 million.

There was a reminder of the Civil War in a letter from one Richmonder. The letter said: "Sir, Shocked by the unparalleled *Titanic* disaster, the American people are comforted by an object lesson to be recorded in the annals of history. John Jacob Astor, a Northern millionaire, stands aside to allow some women to be saved. Major Archibald Butt, representative of our government and a Southerner, stands side by side with Colonel Astor and faces and accepts death, thereby illustrating the glorious manhood of race and our innate chivalry." In a final comment, the writer suggested, "Let us toast Astor and Butt."

As a reminder of the recent disaster, there was a story about icebergs moving into the area where the *Titanic* sank. It was reported that they were being closely watched and wireless reports were keeping the proper authorities advised of their locations. It was further reported that, if necessary, the sea lanes would be moved farther south to avoid another disaster.

And to keep people from profiting from the disaster, the mayor of Boston advised "all the motion picture houses in the city that he would not tolerate the production of *Titanic* disaster pictures."

For two weeks, the Richmond newspapers had covered the loss of the *Titanic* from every conceivable angle. In the days ahead, the story would continue as more information surfaced about that April night when an iceberg turned dreams into nightmares and changed lives forever.

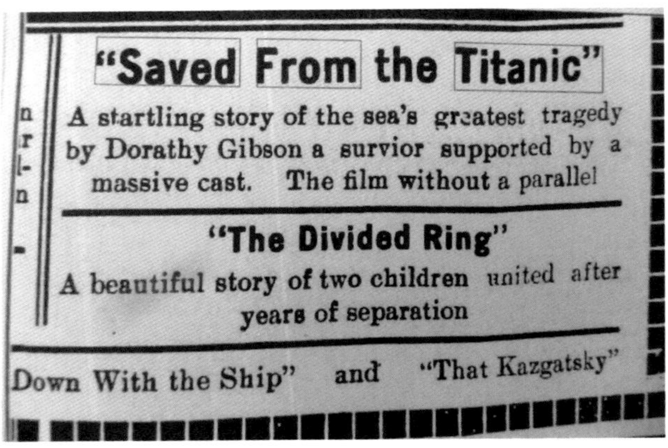

Advertisement for a movie about the *Titanic*. *Author's collection.*

Chapter 26

The Great Ship Sails On

As sank the doom'd Titanic
Beneath the yawning sea.
Its last of earthly music
Was "Nearer, My God, to Thee";
Its notes of Trust inspiring,
Even to its latest breath.
And of a faith triumphant
While facing certain death.
—Duval Porter

After May 1, the primary *Titanic* news concerned the hearings in the United States and England. These hearings revealed many details about that tragic April Sunday night. Other *Titanic* news that tended to stay in the newspaper concerned finding bodies and the funerals of the very wealthy.

For example, the funeral of John Jacob Astor was headline news in Richmond. Every detail of the funeral was reported, including that the casket was kept closed even though Astor's body was in pristine condition. It was reported that his first wife was not present, but his second wife and her family were very much in evidence.

The memorial service for Archibald Butt was attended by 1,500 people. It was noticed that President William Howard Taft had tears in his eyes when he delivered the eulogy for his close friend. President Taft said, "I couldn't prepare anything in advance to say here." He continued, "I tried but

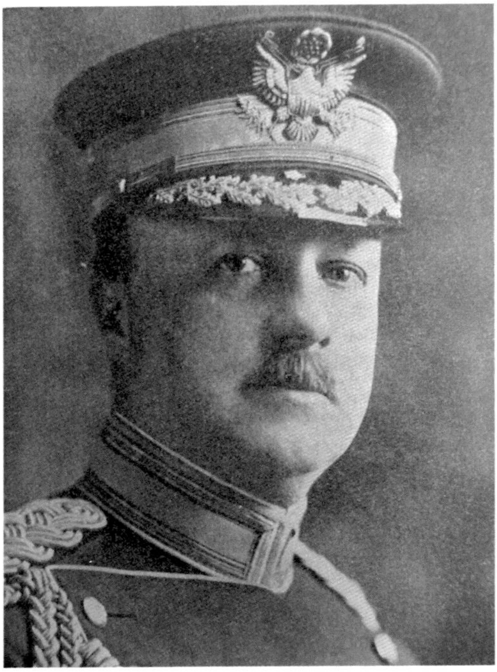

Major Archibald Butt, the military advisor to President William Howard Taft who was lost when the *Titanic* went down. *Courtesy of the Library of Congress.*

couldn't. He was too near me. He was loyal to my predecessor, President Theodore Roosevelt, who selected him to be his military aide, and to me he had become as a son or a brother." President Taft then said, "If Archie could have selected a time to die, he would have chosen the one God gave him."

The funeral service for Isidor Straus was held at Temple Beth El in New York City. Rabbi Samuel Schulman said, "God's ways are not our ways. Therefore, we should not attempt to define His motive in the tragic end of this great person." He then concluded by observing, "What enabled Isidor Straus to do all the things that he accomplished? Our answer must be, 'God blessed him and gave him Ida Straus.' Isidor and Ida Straus were two persons with a single thought. Beloved and adored by each other in life, and in death they were not separated."

The search for bodies ended. Mercifully, the life jackets that were keeping the dead passengers and crew members floating in the Atlantic deteriorated, and their bodies joined the *Titanic* at the bottom of the sea.

The most important news in the months ahead was the release of the reports of the United States Senate and the hearings in England. The report of the United States Senate had several recommendations, including that "all ships must carry sufficient lifeboats for all passengers and each person has to be assigned to a specific lifeboat; two wireless operators must be assigned to all ships; and radio communication must be maintained around the clock." The British inquiry found that the cause of the accident was "brought about by the excessive speed at which the ship was being navigated."

In May 1912, the Richmond newspapers carried the news that the Women of America had begun a campaign to erect the "Women's Titanic

Memorial" in Washington, D.C. For many months, there were stories about the fundraising efforts, and Richmond women were very much involved in this effort. Major donations to the memorial merited a story in the *Times Dispatch.* The memorial was unveiled by Mrs. William Howard Taft on May 26, 1931. The inscription on the monument is as follows:

To the brave men
Who perished
In the wreck
Of the Titanic
April 15, 1912.
They gave their
Lives that women
And children
May be saved.

Erected by the
Women of America

The story of the loss of the *Titanic* has not ended. Frequently, it is referred to in the media as an example of many bad things—and perhaps a few good things. A favorite phrase is "arranging deck chairs on the *Titanic*," which suggests you are engaged in a worthless endeavor. The discovery of the sunken *Titanic* by Dr. Robert Ballard in 1985 once again focused attention on the loss of the ship, as did the 100th anniversary of its sinking in 2012. There have also been a number of movies and many books that have kept the story of the *Titanic* alive.

Across the years, all of the survivors of the *Titanic* have passed away. Only the decaying hulk of the ship remains, and in time, it, too, will disappear. Yet the story of the *Titanic* is without end. The horrible stories of death and destruction, life and death, pain and suffering, courage and cowardice, arrogance and humility, prayers and cursing, tears and gunshots are as captivating today as when they occurred in 1912. The lessons learned from this disaster have saved many lives, and people are no longer willing to proclaim something as invincible.

For many years, the United States Coast Guard dropped a wreath on the *Titanic*'s grave on the anniversary of its loss. As part of the ceremony, the Coast Guard pilot would speak these words: "On behalf of the United States Coast Guard…we cast this wreath. We now pause for a moment of silence to

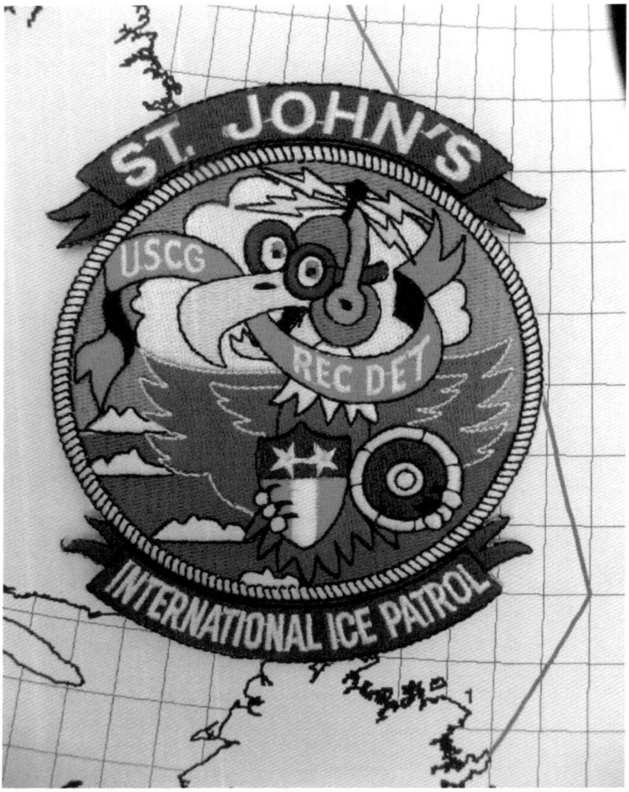

Left: International Ice Patrol patch. *Author's collection.*

Below: A Coast Guard C-100 aircraft overflies an iceberg during an ice patrol in the Arctic Ocean. *Courtesy of the United States Coast Guard.*

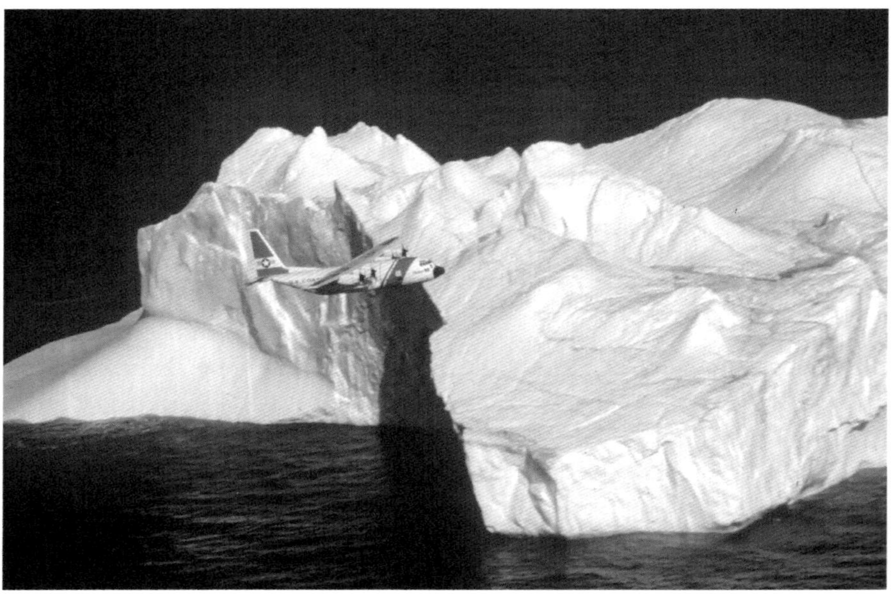

reflect on the event that occurred at this place in the North Atlantic." Another reminder of the *Titanic* is the International Ice Patrol that is constantly watching for icebergs so ships will no longer destroy themselves on a mountain of ice. And for the survivors of the *Titanic*, this hymn was written.

To the tune of "O God, Our Help in Ages Past."

Lord of the everlasting hills,
God of the boundless sea,
Help us through all the shocks of fate
To keep our trust in Thee.

When nature's unrelenting arm
Sweep us like withes away,
Maker of man, be Thou our strength
And our eternal stay.

When blind, insensate, heartless force
Puts out our passing breath,
Make us to see Thy guiding light,
In darkness and in death.

Beneath the roll of soundless waves
Our best and bravest lie;
Give us to feel their spirits live
Immortal in the sky.

We are Thy children, frail and small.
Formed of the lowly soil
Comfort our bruised and bleeding souls,
Father and Lord and God.

—Hall Caine

Perhaps, if you look at the Atlantic Ocean on a cold, starlit night and listen carefully, you will hear a heavenly chorus singing "Nearer, My God, to Thee." And you might see a vision of a magnificent ocean liner sailing on a sea where there are no icebergs, no destruction, no death and only a calm sea reflecting the twinkling stars, a full moon and the blazing lights of a ship named *Titanic.*

Bibliography

Books

Adams, Moody. *The Titanic's Last Hero.* Yucca Valley, CA: Rocklin Press, 2012.

Baker, Alan. *The Vikings.* Hoboken, NJ: John Wiley and Sons, Inc., 2004.

Beesley, Lawrence. *I Survived the Titanic*. Gloucestershire, UK: Amberly Publishing, 2013.

Biel, Steven. *Down with the Old Canoe.* New York: W.W. Norton and Company, 1996.

Butler, Daniel Allen. *The Other Side of the Night.* Philadelphia: Casemate, 2009.

———. *Unsinkable.* Philadelphia: Da Capo Press, 1998.

Carroll, Yvonne. *A Hymn for Eternity*. Stroud, UK: The History Press, 2011.

Davenport-Hines, Richard. *Voyages of the Titanic.* New York: HarperCollins, 2012.

De Kerbrech, Richard. *Ships of the White Star Line*. Hersham, Surrey, UK: Allan Publishing Co., 2009.

Eaton, John P., and Charles A. Haas. *Titanic: Destination Disaster.* Newbury Park, UK: Haynes Publishing, 2011.

Everett, Marshall. *Wreck of the Titanic*. New York: Harper Design, n.d.

Heyer, Paul. *Titanic Legacy*. Westport, CT: Praeger, 1995.

Lord, Walter. *The Night Lives On.* New York: William Morrow and Company, Inc., 1986.

———. *A Night to Remember.* New York: Henry Holt and Company, 1955.

Matsen, Brad. *Titanic's Last Secrets*. New York: Twelve, 2008.

Maxtone-Graham, John. *Titanic Tragedy*. New York: W.W. Norton, Co., 2011.
McCabe, James. *The Birds of Ill-Omen*. N.p.: Amazon Digital Books, 2012.
Mowbray, Jay Henry. *Sinking of the Titanic*. Harrisburg, PA: The Miner Company, 1912.
Pellegrino, Charles. *Farewell, Titanic.* Hoboken, NJ: John Wiley and Sons, Inc., 2012.
Pipe, John. *Titanic: A Very Peculiar History*. Brighton, East Sussex, UK: Salariya Book Company, Ltd., 2012.
Rossignol, Ken. *Titanic Poetry, Music and Stories.* California, MD: Huggins Point Publishing Co., 2013.
Stephenson, H.W. *Nearer, My God, to Thee.* London: Lindsey Press, 1922.
Turner, Steve. *The Band That Played On*. Nashville: Thomas Nelson, 2011.
Wade, Wynn Craig. *The Titanic: End of a Dream*. New York: Wade Publishers, Inc., 1979.
Ward, Greg. *The Rough Guide to the Titanic*. London: Rough Guides, Ltd., 2012.

NEWSPAPERS

Evening Journal, April 1, 1912–May 1, 1912.
News Leader, April 1, 1912– May 1, 1912.
Richmond Dispatch, April 1, 1912–May 1, 1912.
Richmond Planet, April 1, 1912–May 1, 1912.
Times Dispatch, April 1, 1912–May 1, 1912.

About the Author

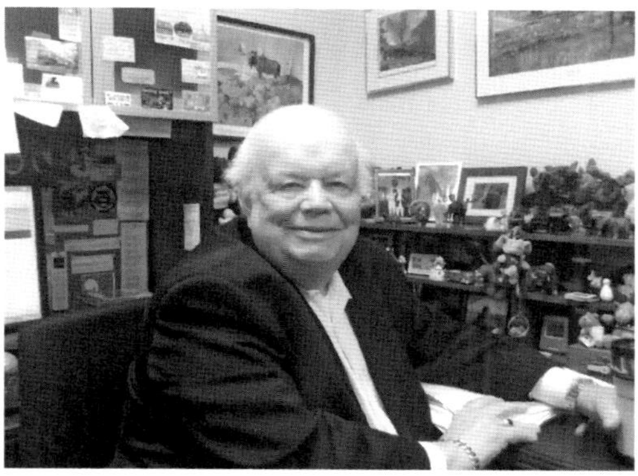

Dr. Walter S. Griggs Jr. is a professor at Virginia Commonwealth University in Richmond, Virginia, where he teaches law. He has also taught history courses in the Honors College, including a course on the *Titanic*. He holds a master's degree from the University of Richmond, a juris doctorate from the University of Richmond School of Law and a doctorate from the College of William and Mary in Virginia. Griggs has written the following books published by The History Press: *The Collapse of Richmond's Church Hill Tunnel*, *The Hidden History of Richmond* and *World War II Richmond, Virginia*. He has also written books on the Civil War, fire departments and moose. He was awarded the Jefferson Davis Medal for his Civil War books and articles. Griggs is married to the former Frances Pitchford, who is fortunately a retired English teacher and librarian. She edits and proofs his work. He is also fortunate to have a daughter, Cara, who is a reference archivist for the Library of Virginia. Walter Griggs and his family live in Richmond, Virginia.